Authoritative Revelations on Tipping
Guidelines & Solutions

Edwin F. Jablonski and Barbara R. Wohlfahrt

PRIME CONSULTANTS, INC..
P.O. Box 1935
Wausau, Wisconsin 54402

authorHOUSE™

1663 LIBERTY DRIVE, SUITE 200
BLOOMINGTON, INDIANA 47403
(800) 839-8640
WWW.AUTHORHOUSE.COM

First published by AuthorHouse 2/13/2006

ISBN: 1-4208-6942-6 (sc)

Library of Congress Control Number: 2005906084

Printed in the United States of America
Bloomington, Indiana

This book is printed on acid-free paper.

Library of Congress Cataloging in Publication Data
Jablonski, Edwin F., 1925-
Authoritative Revelations on Tipping.
Includes Index.
1. Tipping. 2. The Public Responds. 3. Legal Aspects.
I. Wohlfahrt, Barbara R., 1947 -
II. Title.

ACKNOWLEDGEMENTS

Portions of this book were reproduced with permission from the following:

"Service is an Honorable Profession" by Ed Solomon
"Meeting News" a Gralla Production, Peter Shure
"Dear Abby" by Abigail Van Buren
Joseph Biedrzycki
Fred A. Robbins
James Warner (Illustrations)
John E. Schein (Founder of Tippers International, Ltd.)
(deceased)
D. Lehman

Table of Contents

To Dorothy, Tim and John

PREFACE

Today, in the United States and throughout the rest of the world, we are living in an era when tipping is a way of life. It has almost become mandatory to the extent that a person feels guilty if you do not tip properly or do not tip at all.

Tipping has become a significant item in everyone's budget, especially those who travel extensively. Based on market analysis, just in the service categories of taxicabs, eating and drinking establishments, hotels and other lodgings, beauty shops and barber shops, there were over 400,000 of these U.S. establishments, with about 6,000,000 employees with a payroll of over $36,000,000,000 in the mid 1980's. This figure continues to increase because our country has become service oriented. Over $5,000,000,000 was being spent each year in tips during the mid 1980's and we figure that amount has increased accordingly.

It is no wonder that our government has studied tipping in depth, and has enacted several tax measures designed to improve reporting of tip income. To secure greater tax compliance, Congress passed the Tax Equity and Fiscal Responsibility Act of 1982 (TEFRA) as discussed in Chapter 16.

This book, "Authoritative Revelations on Tipping" has been conceived to bring proper definition for education and reference on the subject of tipping. Its authors have been advising customers (tippers and tippees) for many years through a service organization called "Tippers International, Ltd." This book is a complete compendium on the subject of tipping, and presents in detail a basic philosophy on the subject, detailed special considerations for all businesses in which tipping is a common practice, and the particular aspects of tipping, worldwide, by country. The considerations of the "Tippee" are presented as well as those of the "Tipper."

Throughout the book the authors have used the "Robby Tipper" symbol, originated by "Tippers International, Ltd." to identify the highlights of the text. This symbol meaningfully depicts a service professional ready to serve you.

We suggest anyone concerned with tipping read Chapters 1 thru 4 to develop a broad understanding of the subject, and the authors' philosophy. Chapters 5 thru 8 present detailed advice by type of business. Chapter 9 provides specific information for convention and meeting planners. Chapter 10 is designed to serve the international traveler with information classified by country. Chapters 11 and 12 explain, with examples, tipping philosophy in various situations. Chapter 13 outlines for the service professional what they should provide their customers in the way of good service. Chapter 14 considers the subject of tipping from the woman's point of view, and Chapter 15 identifies the special considerations of the disabled traveler. Chapter 16 considers in depth the tax implications of tipping. Chapter 17 gives an analysis of the book.

We are confident that anyone concerned with tipping will profit from the basic philosophy presented, and the details applicable to his particular situation, either as "Tipper" or "Tippee."

ABOUT THE AUTHORS

Edwin Jablonski and Barbara Wohlfahrt, owners of Prime Consultants with offices in Wausau, Wisconsin, Phoenix, Arizona, and Orlando, Florida, have again pooled their expertise to present the second edition on tipping named "Authoritative Revelations on Tipping – Guidelines and Solutions."

Edwin Jablonski is President and a founder of Prime Consultants, a consulting firm. He also holds a position as President of a newly organized architectural aluminum window company. He falls in the category of an entrepreneur by being instrumental in organizing six new companies in the past 45 years. His executive positions and the travel requirements of those positions have exposed him to numerous tipping situations, while entertaining, attending seminars and expositions, participating in trade shows and planning sales meetings. His five visits to Europe have given him the exposure to tipping in other countries.

Lastly, Ed was selected into the Packer Hall of Fame as the third honorary fan in the year 2000, followed by a selection in the Visa Hall of Fans in Canton. He is presently a member of Pro Football's Ultimate Fan Association. He is a graduate of the University of Wisconsin at Madison, Wisconsin with a Bachelor's Degree of Business Administration from the School of Commerce.

Barbara Wohlfahrt is a founding member of Prime Consultants and has held Executive Vice President positions in three different companies. Presently she is working in real estate. These positions and also her extensive worldwide travels to Europe on five different occasions have provided her with a great deal of exposure to tipping in many different countries and situations. She is a graduate of the University of Wisconsin at Madison, Wisconsin with a Bachelor's of Science Degree from the School of Mechanical Engineering.

The authors have been officers of Tipper's International, LTD. (TI) for over 20 years and some of the copy in their book relates to the research of this company. John Schein founded this organization in 1968 and we joined him in the 1980's. The organization has become inactive since John Schein's death in 2000. We have contributed information for articles published in over 200 newspapers, magazines, newsletters and periodicals around the world. We appeared as guests on many radio and television programs, including "P.M. Magazine," "Good Morning America," "To Tell The Truth" and "MacNeil-Lehrer Report." That is the reason we consider ourselves the true authority on tipping.

PART I
Why Tipping

CHAPTER 1

***

Rules, Systems and Responsibilities

Why do we have tipping today? It is a system that works, that's why! It has worked for hundreds of years and all indications are that it will continue as long as people require services. The practice has spread from its earliest recorded beginnings in ancient Europe to most of the contemporary free world, because this system is based on the simple generosity of people who give tips and the self assurance of those who work to receive them.

The growth of tipping practices occurred despite early opposition, and its success today is sufficient evidence that people will reward others for well performed personal services. If you are one of the millions who feel comfortable rewarding good work performances, then you are a good TIPPER, and a world of good service is waiting for you.

TIPPEES are the other people. They work in the service professions and their income depends on the response of tipping customers to their services. They believe in their abilities enough to accept tipping as their incentive for serving you well.

There is usually a mutual respect existing between tippers and tippees, and as long as givers and receivers both recognize the values tipping holds for all parties, the system will continue to thrive.

Another important characteristic that makes this free enterprise system work is that tipping is voluntary. Money is paid for the delivery of services. There is no obligation for any customer to give a tip, and the person who gives one exercises the freedom of the final word. Tipping is a free will decision that benefits the participants in ways that transcend the amount of money involved. It is a powerful form of communication. The tippee gains the immediate satisfaction of knowing the service was appreciated, while the tipper experiences both the human glow from expressing generosity and the freedom of being the judge in the tipping situation. These simple concepts explain the success and future of tipping.

The beauty of tipping is its simplicity. It is a basic economic relationship on a human scale. This book aims to keep it that way while providing you with solutions to the complete range of tipping problems. It should provide a better understanding of what tipping means to everybody. Some say tipping is an art, while others call it a necessity. However you view tipping, if you follow some clear rules and thoughtful systems to determine your tips, you can make the process easy, effective and fair.

RULES

Rule No. 1 — Let the Tip Do the Talking

Let the tip do the talking is the most important rule of tipping. Make it a personal resolution never to say anything more than a simple thank you for good service if you leave a tip. Never express your dissatisfaction whether you leave a tip or not. Remember, your tip speaks much louder than words. It saves the all important final word for you, the tipper, and it avoids any misunderstandings. The amount of the tip or the lack of money you leave behind says it all.

Consider this example. A waiter we know who served dinner to a customer advised us how that customer lavished praise on him  during and after dinner for the magnificent service he had given. Later, when the customer had gone, the waiter found a very modest tip on the table. This tip was far less than what he was accustomed to receiving from the restaurant's other patrons. The waiter said that his first thought was that the praise the man had given him was intended to be a tongue in cheek insult

4

for the service. This incident hurt the waiter who spent considerable time wondering what he had done wrong until the man returned to the restaurant for a meal. Only then did the waiter realize that the man indeed had meant to praise him, but was simply a modest tipper. Had the customer been more discreet with his praise in the first place, the waiter would have graciously accepted the tip as a modest one, and no more thought would have been given the matter. If less had been said, considerable mental anguish could have been avoided.

Saying too much the other way can also backfire. Avoid the mistake of verbalizing your dissatisfaction as well. The moment you utter a word of displeasure to a serving person, you open the way for escalating the unfortunate situation. Your words, once spoken, invite a response, which may either become an argument, an unnecessary discussion, or an avalanche of embarrassing excuses and apologies. The argument is obviously unwanted. A discussion often ends in compromises you may not have anticipated. Worst of all, apologies have a way of bringing out the old softie in people, and you may wind up leaving more of a tip than you had intended, and certainly one that was undeserved.

The tip or no tip is always the best way of reserving the final word for yourself. Always let the tip do the talking.

Rule No. 2 — Tip the Server, Never the House

It is a real dilemma when the food was terrible but the service was great. What do you decide? The answer is no easier when the reverse is true, good food but bad service. The rule to tip the server and not the establishment resolves the issue. Base the tip on the performance of the serving person and you will never go wrong.

Think about who is being rewarded for what. The person serving you seldom has control over anything but the tasks they perform on your behalf. A chambermaid is not responsible for the furniture in a hotel room. A cabbie has little control over the model and condition of the car the company gives him to drive. A waiter can send poorly prepared food back to the kitchen only so many times. Rarely will you find occasions when the people who serve you control the quality of the product they deliver. That responsibility lies with management.

So, reward the house by patronizing it again, which gives management another chance. Reward the server on the basis of service.

Rule No. 3 — Tip for Today, Never for Future Service

The process of tipping has made many people feel defensive. There is no cause for such feelings, especially if you live by this rule to tip for the service being provided now.

Most of us have at some time pondered what effect not leaving a tip might have the next time we visit a place. This occurs often to people who are frequent patrons of particular businesses. The reasons for these situations are familiar ones. You feel compelled to patronize establishments because of their location or convenient hours of operation, but you do so despite the employees who serve you, or better yet, the ones who fail to serve you. You usually leave a tip, right? You must realize that you are tipping not because of the fine service you have received, but rather as a defense against worse service the next time. Has the service improved? Probably not, but you go on tipping anyway.

There are variations of defensive tipping that even the most dissatisfied customers may practice. For example, you may find yourself being served as a regular customer and the service is poor. There may be many reasons for this, but you become personally involved and leave a tip regardless of the quality of your server's performance.

No good will be attained in either of the above cases if you yield to defensive feelings. Stick to your guns. At the least, modify your tip. No service person will have incentive to overcome their feelings or whatever the reason for the poor service unless it is communicated to them in the most meaningful way, the tip. Dwindling tips will benefit you and the establishment by encouraging deliverers of poor service to find more suitable employment if they cannot improve their performance. Tip only for today and for service received, never for future service. This is the best guarantee of good service in the future.

The real art of tipping flowers when neither the server nor the customer allows the business relationship to reach the personal level where bruised feelings can affect it. But, friendships can develop between the service person and the consumer when the same establishment is patronized on a regular basis. This is a natural process and should be handled the same as when a relative becomes the service person, regardless of the type of business — restaurant, beauty parlor, barber shop, etc.

The fair way to handle these situations would be to apply the rules of tipping and treat these service people as you would any other. However, if you feel that this service person should be treated differently, and you would like to be on the generous side, you might establish a flat tip to give, regardless of the cost of the service. This establishes a pattern and the service person can expect this amount for their services every time you are served. In many cases, the joy of just seeing and serving you is part of the compensation for this friendship, and also knowing that their ability to create this goodwill will help the establishment's owner.

Be careful not to let this type of tipping get out of hand. This relationship could result in hurt feelings if service slips. This situation could also become embarrassing to the service person or the customer. It is, of course, safer to just apply the rules of tipping and be generous, but discreet.

Rule No. 4 — Pause, Evaluate and Calculate on Merit

Tipping, like anything else, requires a certain amount of time and deliberation until your pattern is established. The few seconds it takes to evaluate each tipping transaction is important to the success of the system because there are many forces working to make you leave hastily calculated amounts, sometimes more than you should. If you develop the habit of quietly figuring out your tip and make certain the correct change is left, you will accurately express your feelings and also help discourage intimidating tricks service people sometimes use to beat the system.

No one has the right to rush you. In a restaurant, a taxi or a car wash, you are the customer, and you are paying for the product. You should set the pace and not allow anyone to rush you.

Before looking at some of the tricks you may encounter, you should realize that serving people who adopt a sunny, pleasant and helpful attitude are by no means trying to trick you into leaving a bigger tip. In fairness to them, it is one of the objectives of the system to develop precisely such behavior. Their efforts should be appreciated.

Your evaluation procedure will help avoid tip intimidation. The frequent example of this occurs when the server extends an open palm awaiting a tip. Avoid handing out the first coins or bills you reach in your haste to fill the waiting hand. Pause! Evaluate! Calculate on merit! Give only the appropriate amount for the service you have received. Some aggressive service people may not accept your terms for the task they have performed. They may continue to hold their palm open with your tip in sight while adopting a questioning stare as if to say "Is this all?" or "Haven't you forgotten something?" This technique may be attempted even when your tip was adequate. This is intimidation at its worst and should be handled in an equally intimidating way. Stare back. Hold your ground. Such aggressive behavior spoils the tipping system for everyone.

Serving people also find ways of making subtle references to gratuities left by other customers. They may exclaim their pleasure at large tips or grumble about small ones. This technique is directed at you to indicate what will please them. They hope your generous nature will force you to seek their approval by leaving a larger tip. Just remember this is the cart pulling the horse. You are the evaluator. It is when you allow yourself to be intimidated that the system breaks down. There is no point in giving good tips for poor service.

To make tipping easier, always carry enough change and small bills to make sure you are never forced to give more than necessary for lack of small change. Service personnel sometimes recognize this too. No one knows where it started, but experienced service professionals have been known to train newcomers to leave change

8

in amounts and denominations that will encourage unintended generosity.   Amid your change you may discover half dollars instead of quarters, or five dollar bills instead of singles. This may occur as a result of the check total, but you are not required to abide by what is there. Rely on your rule. Pause! Evaluate! Calculate on merit! Leave the appropriate amount and do not hesitate to ask for smaller bills if necessary. Depart knowing you acted fairly. Why allow yourself to be intimidated?

Rule No. 5 — Tip Discreetly, Never Dramatize Your Reward

The purpose of a tip or gratuity is a reward for good work done by the professional service person. It should never be dramatized.

In taxicabs or situations with porters, bellmen or others where payment for service must be handed directly to the recipient, do it simply and routinely. A simple thank you or keep the change is drama enough. More than that becomes pretentious. Demonstrative tipping calls for attention and tends to evoke an unnecessary display of humility from otherwise capable professional service people. Allow them their dignity. If you say anything, keep it simple, quiet and private.

Tips left at tables should either be placed on the tray provided or discreetly tucked under a plate. Rely on your supply of change and small bills to pay the tip before you leave the table. If you leave to pay the cashier before tipping or to obtain change, you are forced to return to the table for the sole purpose of rewarding the server. This calls undue attention to the tip and could tend to intimidate nearby customers. Although you may have received good service and are willing to reward it generously, this does not mean others enjoyed the same good fortune. If the busboy has already begun to clear your table, this can also complicate getting your tip to the waiter. Such extra effort is unnecessary and tends to complicate the tipping process.

Remember that the table where you sit is the reference point between you and the waiter who may not know your name. Waiters remember what their customers look like, the things said to them, and the table where their customers sat. They will recall the tip even if circumstances force you to return to the table. Your objective is getting the tip to the right person. If you leave it with the cashier, you risk having the wrong person receive it because the cashier can easily confuse the table number or waiter's name.

Another awkward situation occurs when you decide to add the tip to the check or pay by credit card. If the waiter handles the transaction at your table, communication is clearer and the service person will obtain the gratuity from the cashier. If you take the check or credit card to the cashier, however, you again run the risk of the waiter being short changed and not knowing whether you were pleased or satisfied with the service. If you are compelled to complete the transaction with the cashier, you should mention to the waiter that you are including the tip in the payment. This can be accomplished by sign language when you catch the waiter's eye. Point to the check in your hand and then toward the cashier, nodding your head in that direction as if to say — pick up your tip at the cash register. Serving people learn this discreet pantomime quickly, and you can convey the message without interrupting their service to other customers.

When you speak to the cashier there are some comments you can make while paying that will make you feel you have done your best to insure your waiter gets the tip. One frequently used technique is to ask the cashier "Let's see now, who was my waiter?" The cashier will normally take a second look at the check and give you the name. That second look is important. You have succeeded in pointing out that a tip has been added, and this assures that it will reach the waiter. Cashiers are honest and must maintain a harmonious working relationship with the serving staff, who will check with the cashier to make sure tips are received.

Still another way to insure that your server knows you appreciated the service without dramatizing the matter is to politely ask the cashier to convey your thanks to the waiter. Restaurants often have a system of pooling tips to be shared by all the service personnel at the end of each shift. In cases of this kind, when you pay by credit card, the waiter has no other means of knowing your appreciation except through a word of thanks relayed by the cashier.

Rule No. 6 — Guest Tipper Rule

One of life's pleasures is having someone else pick up the tab. In such situations many people will volunteer to cover the tip. Such responses to the generosity of others can lead to mistakes in the world of tipping unless we have the necessary information. The Guest Tipper Rule is simply to pay the tip only if you know the amount of the check.

The reason why is important to you, your host, the server, and the tipping merit system. If you guess at the amount, you are likely to overtip, which serves no purpose. Moreover, you do not wish to embarrass your host by leaving too little. Often there are items on the check you were not aware of, such as extra drinks, special beverages, desserts, or wines. Consequently, the only correct way to proceed is to ask the amount of the check from either your host or the waiter. If you find out from your host, it is still proper to inform your waiter that you are leaving the tip. That way, if your host happens to be the last of the big tippers, the waiter will know it was you who recognized the true value of his service, and your host will be exonerated. This is the least you can do in return for a free meal.

Rule No. 7 — No Tip on Top — The Service Charge Rule

Never tip on top of a service charge because the service charge that is added to your bill already goes to the service professional. We have surveys indicating that 72% of the American public feels service is worse where service charges are added and that 91% prefer the tipping system. However, some scattered restaurants in the United States do add service charges to the bill. Some people consider this system, which is commonly practiced abroad, to be high handed, but it is legal if due notice is given on the menu. Always check. Under the service charge system, 15% or more is automatically added to the tab whether the customer believes the gratuity is earned or not. It adds insult to injury when an unsuspecting guest looks at the total bill and leaves another 15%, not realizing that a service charge was already included. No reports have ever reached us of such double tips being returned to customers. Service charges do not allow you the final word in evaluating the tasks that have been performed for you. For the unsuspecting, tips on tips are absurd.

There are times, however, when service charges are appropriate. Banquets, catered events and large parties are examples of gatherings where normal tipping procedures should be dropped. At such functions service is normally less personal, and these events require far more serving personnel because all guests must be served simultaneously. Time pressure, increased personnel, and larger numbers of guests are all good reasons for making the service charge the logical means of rewarding waiters and waitresses at these kinds of events. The hosts or caterers usually clarify that the service charge is included.

Often when you attend an event, you pay the club treasurer or pick up your dinner tickets from a cashier. Frequently the service charges are included in the price of your meal. If you are not sure, ask. Never pay without asking and by all means never leave a tip without knowing if one has already been included.

Overseas tours and domestic travel packages usually include gratuities for meals and transportation in the price. Remember, no tip on top. Always make sure you understand which of the various functions in the package include the tips. Chances are the serving people will not know or wish to tell. Rely on your tour guide or travel agent for valid information.

SYSTEMS

We present here a brief discussion of the different formulas most often used to calculate tips. These methods will be examined in more detail in Chapter 4.

Percentage Systems

The most common method used to determine the gratuity is to take a percentage of the bill. No one can really say why or where this practice began, but it is widespread and it seems that the majority of tippers prefer using percentages to simplify the system. Imagine how difficult tipping would be if you had to remember a different fee for each of the many tipping situations you encounter. The percentage concept eliminates the need for the extra memory storage otherwise required. Of course, percentages can only be used in those situations where a specific price is given for goods or services.

Percentages can be calculated by the use of one of the following formulas:

1. *What You Receive is What You Leave Formula* With this method the customary rate of 15% is increased or decreased depending on the spectrum of services provided. For example, if the restaurant provides customary services, 15% is appropriate, while in a gourmet restaurant 20% would be called for; but in some cafeteria establishments, a 5-10% tip would be satisfactory.

2. *Ten Plus or Minus Five Formula*
To apply this formula, determine 10% of the bill and then take half again and add or subtract to figure a tip of 5% for poor service, 10% for fair service or 15% for good service.

3. *One for Seven Formula*
Divide the total amount of the bill by seven to arrive at a tip of about 14%. Add a small amount more if you wish to tip the usual 15%.

4. *Times Sales Tax Formula*
To use this formula you must first determine the sales tax levied in the state. If this tax is 5% multiply the sales tax figure on the bill by three to arrive at a 15% tip. Change your multiplier to arrive at other percentages.

Flat Tip System

In situations where no specific price is given (like for the services of a chambermaid), a flat tip should be given. Flat tips can be arrived at in several ways. People who prefer not to give a percentage of the total bill often give a flat amount, regardless of the service provided or the size of the bill. These tips are usually based on even money amounts, such as one or two dollars.

Flat tips are often given to bus drivers or travel guides. The group will often agree on what amount is to be given to the guide or driver. Flat tips are sometimes used at conventions, meetings and seminars where an amount per attendee is agreed upon ahead of time by the customer and the establishment's manager. Suggested amounts to be given in particular situations are provided throughout this book.

RESPONSIBILITIES

Accept good service people as special. Success at what you do in any field takes special talent, and people who care about good service soon learn that those who succeed in the serving professions excel in many important human qualities. They are alert to what you say and how you say it. They are forthright and honest in answering your questions. They are sensitive to your needs, likes and dislikes. They learn to sense when you are in a hurry or wish to relax. They adjust quickly when they recognize that you are businesslike or jovial. They become skilled at moving efficiently through crowded streets or restaurants and exhibit amazing dexterity in manipulating heavy bags, bulky trays of hot foods, carts, wagons and vehicles. Often, as if by some kind of magic, they do all this while smiling and carrying on a thoughtful conversation with you.

Porters, waiters, cab drivers, doormen, chambermaids, parking attendants — they all have a right to be recognized for the vitally important work they do in every corner of the world. These people are the ones who bring you in out of the rain, move your goods, make you comfortable, get you where you're going, bring what you need, and take away what you don't need.   They watch for your safety and help make you comfortable. This is service with a capital S, and it deserves everyone's respect. You will receive the greatest rewards from tipping if you recognize the talents that serving professionals share with you and recognize these people as special.

CHAPTER 2

***

History of Tipping

Tipping seems to have originated back in the days of the feudal lords. It was a token of generosity bestowed by a wealthy person on someone of lowly estate, such as a serf. When journeying lords would meet groups of leering beggars along their paths, they would toss the beggars handfuls of coins in an attempt to purchase a safe passage.

Origin of Tipping

The origin of the term "tip" has been traced back to England in the 16th Century when the local gentry would gather in coffee shops, known as penny universities, to exchange opinions and ideas. Brass bound boxes were placed at the door of the shop and coins were dropped in "To Insure Promptitude." And so the word tip, based on the first letters of the three words on the boxes or bowls, became a common way of referring to the gratuities. And in London coffee houses a couple of centuries ago, the customers started giving waiters notes writing the words "To Insure Promptitude" with coins attached.

This way of getting service spread quickly throughout Europe. It seemed to thrive in lands where there was a servant class. But it wasn't until after the Civil War that it started catching on in the United States. Until then, European travelers to the United States would write of their amazement in finding that they were not expected to tip in America. It has been said that tipping had not caught on in the United States because the country had no servants. Instead, the waiter and the coachman regarded themselves as employees and weren't interested in tips.

Tipping Takes Hold in America

Newly affluent Americans traveling in Europe found out they had to tip. So, when they returned home to the United States, they began tipping to show that they had been abroad and knew the latest customs of Europe.

Yet even as late as 1900, the waiter, the bellboy and the Pullman porter were almost the only individuals in America who were regularly accepting tips. And even if they weren't tipped, they didn't give any indication that they despised the customer for failing to tip.

But the nouveau riche promoted the practice of tipping to an ever widening range of employees by using tips to purchase special services that others less well off could not afford. Soon, would be up-and-comers with less money started imitating them. And the craze for keeping up with the Joneses and copying the ways of Europe took hold firmly, and tipping became a way of life. In fact, America became known as the land of bigger and better tipping. We started tipping for reasons Europeans hadn't even thought of. Well dressed Americans traveling in Europe became known as easy marks for outstretched palms.

Tipping Survives Opposition

But, about 1905 tipping ran into organized resistance. An organization called the Anti-Tipping Society of America was formed by more than 100,000 traveling salesmen. And, largely as a result of their efforts, tipping was actually outlawed in the states of Mississippi, Georgia, South Carolina, Tennessee, Arkansas, Washington and Iowa. However, the opposition was weakened in 1919 when anti-tipping laws were judged to be unconstitutional. And so the stage was set for the reckless spending and extravagant tipping of the Roaring Twenties. Among the notoriously big tippers were gangland's nouveau riche and Hollywood stars. It is said that when a picture was finished, the stars would tip everyone who took part in the production, with tips as high as $500 or more.

The depression years slowed down the practice of tipping because few people could spare a dime. But the custom was revived during and immediately following World War II. In fact, scarce bartenders and waiters were able to move easily from one high tipping spot to another. In order to keep their employees, even private clubs found themselves in the position of having to give up their policy against tipping.

Some restaurants have tried to ban tipping by substituting a straight service percentage. But, often, customers automatically or absentmindedly leave a tip in addition to paying the service charge. Also, this involuntary added amount takes away the freedom of choice from the customer. Even though the service charge approach has caught on in European restaurants, it doesn't appear likely to replace tipping in the United States today. In a survey conducted by Tippers International, a very high percentage of those questioned said they do not think an automatic service charge should replace tipping. Over two-thirds said they thought service would be worse if tipping were replaced by the automatic charge, and a very small percentage predicted it would be better.

Those opposed to tipping argue it is undemocratic and thus un-American. It is enslaving and degrading for the one being tipped, they say. They also point out that some of the most professional and courteous service comes from those people who are not tipped, such as airline attendants, bankers, insurance agents, store clerks and public officials. It is argued that receiving a healthy salary rather than tips promotes professionalism.

On the other hand, the livelihood of service people depends to a large extent on tipping. Without your tips, they couldn't exist on their wages alone. And, by compensating service people through tips rather than a straight salary, you encourage good service.

Whether you agree with tipping or not, today most of us feel obligated to tip.

Stories of Tipping

Through the years, many interesting stories about tipping have been told. From merry olde England comes the story of Robin Hood and the Sheriff of Nottingham. Robin Hood is said to have stolen from the rich to give to the poor. And the Sheriff of Nottingham would receive "tips" from wealthy travelers to assure them safe passage through Sherwood Forest. Also, these travelers, always being in a hurry to avoid Robin Hood, would tip the proprietors of the establishments they stopped at along the way in order to receive prompt service.

Originally a tip was usually a dime, but substantially larger tips have been given. There is a story of an oil promoter who had  tremendous service and lavish attention bestowed on him in New York's finest restaurants. This "man about town" had a unique way of tipping — he rewarded the restaurant staff by letting them in on his new oil drillings. He gave them the opportunity to buy stock in his enterprises at par value and sometimes below. Clutching their certificates, they awaited the big day when they would all strike it rich. But, in the meantime, and unknown to the expectant waiters, federal and city investigators and prosecuting attorneys noticed that the big tipper wasn't bothering to look for oil. Actually he had only a small piece of property and he didn't even have any drilling equipment. Facing exposure and a possible jail sentence, he followed his lawyer's advice and started drilling wells to try to give legitimacy to his sham. Much to his surprise, he struck oil. But, our big tipper still didn't forget the waiters. No, he went to them, told them his wells were failures and begged for sympathy. He said that he couldn't let his mistakes cost them money and for half price, he would buy back their stocks. Of course, they jumped at the chance. Only later did they learn about the oilman's good fortune.

There is also the story of the old bell captain giving advice to the new trainee. He told the trainee that he would be dealing with two kinds of couples. The first would be married and he suggested that not too much time be wasted on them because the size of the tip has already been established in the husband's mind. However, with luck the trainee would occasionally get an unmarried couple. For them, money is no object and all they want is to get into their room and get the bellboy out. He told the trainee in this case to stall for time, checking the windows, the closets and the water in the bathroom. The longer you remain, the more nervous the man will become and finally, in desperation, he'll shove a fistful of money in your hand if you just agree to leave. The trainee asked the old crony how he would know if the couple were married or not.

The bell captain said that would be easy, the married man usually flops on the bed first, and his wife always checks the closets to see if there are enough hangers. The unmarried man always makes sure the bolt on the door is working and the woman usually starts combing her hair in front of the mirror.

Disputes Over the Origin of "Tip"

Although, as we said before, the word tip is generally agreed to be an acronym for the phrase "to insure promptitude," many people doubt this. It has also been said that tip comes from the Dutch word "tippen" meaning to tap and refers to the tapping sound of a coin when put on a table or tapped against a glass to draw the waiter's attention.

Another origin suggested for the word tip is from the Latin word "stips" which means gift, and is the root of the word stipend. Also, the Oxford Dictionary of English Etymology refers to the term tip as a "rouges cant," or "medieval street talk," meaning hand it over or simply give me money. There is also a phrase in Romany, the language of the gypsies, "tipper me your money" which meant give me your money. From 18th Century England came the phrase "tip me" which meant simply give me.

The word gratuity comes from the Latin word "gratis" which means pleasing, giving of gratitude, full of favor, appreciation. "Gratuitous and Gratis" means done as a favor, or money given to express pleasure at the achievement of another. Gratuity, which was originally a small token, now means a percentage automatically added to a bill.

It is interesting to note that advance tipping, which seems to work best in large cities such as New York, Chicago and San Francisco, has some colloquial names. In Las Vegas nightclubs, for example, up front tipping to get seats at tables at or near the stage, is known locally as a toke. In Chicago, the traditional way of getting things done is to slip a few dollars to someone with influence. This is known as a gentlemen's bribe. However, money will not always get you the best service. In Boston and Minneapolis, family name is what counts. In Atlanta, old-fashioned southern charm and graciousness get results. And in Washington, D.C., connections are what are important.

Wherever tipping started, and no matter what you call a tip, and whether the tip is in the form of money or gift or special acknowledgement, tipping is certainly here to stay and we must all learn to deal with tipping in a gracious and dignified manner.

Historical Background of Restaurant Services

While looking at the history of tipping, it is also interesting to note the historical background of restaurant service itself. Restaurant service is a combination of historical service passed on to us by tradition and modern methods devised to meet the requirements of feeding large numbers of people. The basic service methods used in the United States have come from five countries.

From France comes the method of serving the guest from a food cart or table placed beside the guest. A modification of this is when the guest serves himself from a platter. The American adaption of this type of service is the well known salad cart or salad bar. Also from France comes the method of ordering a meal "a la carte," where each dish is ordered and priced separately.

The English method of service is commonly called host service, because the platters of food are placed in front of the host or hostess, who serves the individual plates. The service person stands to the right of the host. This has been adopted in America as the method used in serving counterclockwise in serving booths.

The system most commonly used in American restaurants for both regular restaurant service and banquet service is an adaptation of the Russian method. The individual food portions are put on the plates in the kitchen, the plates garnished and then served by the service person to the guests in clockwise order.

From the orient comes the method known in the United States as family style. Bowls or platters of food are brought to the table and passed around. Usually the bowl is passed to the guest of honor first. This method is used in most of our homes in America and has also been adopted in some restaurants.

Buffet service is the most ancient of services and comes from the Middle East and Northern Europe where guests originally served and ate from a single cooking pot. The modern restaurant has, as you are aware, greatly increased the number of cooking pots. This is a very popular method of serving large groups of people. It has also been adapted into the cafeteria style of serving.

CHAPTER 3

***

Five Tipping Viewpoints

Here we present the five viewpoints of tipping — The Golden Rule, Service, Inclusive (Mandatory) Tipping, Advance Tipping and Free Tipping. Each viewpoint has positive and negative aspects. Actually, with the ever increasing situations where tipping is expected or required, all of these viewpoints have their appropriate applications. However, the latter viewpoint of free tipping is by far the most widely thought of and used. Always remember that tipping is an art and careful evaluation is the best way to tastefully cope with unfamiliar situations.

The Golden Rule

The Golden Rule as applied to tipping and gratuities is "Do Unto Others as You Would Have Them Do Unto You." This works out great for the tipper, because a tip is supposed to be an optional expression of appreciation for the service received, but it has its limitations. The Rule assumes that everyone thinks and acts the same, that the other person's needs and wants are the same as yours, and that everyone will follow the same concept.

For the tippee, the Golden Rule presents a conflict of interest in many ways. First, the type of service given might not meet the customer's standards and would be reflected in the size of the tip. Second, the same service might exceed another customer's expectations and they would leave a sizeable tip. Third, professional people working in the service trades of the hospitality industry believe serving to be an honorable profession lending prestige in direct proportion to the quality of work done, just as in any other profession. So, when applying the Golden Rule to tipping, the service person is the one who has to bend the rule and apply his professionalism to receive his fair reward. In other words, the service provided may be what the service provider would be comfortable receiving, but the customer may have entirely different standards. So, the Golden Rule only applies to tipping if the service provider is able to interpret the customer's needs accurately.

Now let's take a negative look at the Golden Rule as some people practice it, and change it to read "Do Not Do Unto Others That Which You Would Not Have Them Do Unto You." Now try and apply this new rule and we find a conflict of interest in the future of the tipping program. In this case, tipping would rather be used to express displeasure at service received.

But, let's take a look at a different perspective that would make more sense — "Do Unto Others as They Would Have You Do Unto Them." This brings out the true meaning of the slogan of Tippers International, "What You Receive Is What You Leave" or the first rule of tipping, "Let the Tip Do the Talking." Again, the service professional must be able to sense the type of service expected of them by each individual customer. Then, the Golden Rule applies very well to tipping.

Service

Service is one of the oldest acts of hospitality in existence. Our Tippers International surveys confirm this.

Fifty percent of the people feel that service is the most important criteria for tipping, but we also find that 71% of the people feel obligated to leave a tip for services even though the service does not meet their standards. And almost all the people feel that service people expect to be tipped for their services, whether they perform well or not.

Our surveys show that some people feel or are made to feel obligated to leave a tip, regardless of the service received. In other words, we tend to tip out of habit and perhaps, to avoid embarrassment. You may even fear that failure to tip may result in less than courteous treatment in the future from the same jilted employee. When a tip is taken for granted, or is expected, its purpose of encouraging good service tends to be lost.

People lose out on good service in the future when they fail to use tipping as a way of encouraging good service, but keep tipping about the same no matter what kind of service or treatment they receive. Management loses as well, because the quality of service given by their employees slips, and customers turn away. When this happens, business falters, the service people feel the pinch and can suffer loss of earnings and may even lose their jobs. Management and their employees may never even realize the real reasons for the loss of their business. So, it is important that management put more emphasis on the front of the house with improved service for customers, rather than the back of the houses, where all the food preparation is done. Prompt and courteous service should always be encouraged.

Inclusive (Mandatory) Tipping

Wherever tipping is practiced today, it employs basically one of two concepts, the free tipping system or the inclusive or mandatory tipping system. We should note at this point that even though the word tip and the word gratuity are thought to have the same meanings by most people, they are in fact not the same. Tip means a voluntary gift or payment, while gratuity means a percentage automatically added to a bill. So, we can see that in the free tipping system, the word tip applies. And, in the inclusive or mandatory system, the word gratuity actually is the accurate word to use.

The inclusive or mandatory tipping system refers to a mandatory payment, usually a prescribed percentage which is added to the total. The inclusive gratuity system was first practiced in Europe where it is now a tradition. The rationale for its implementation was based on the premise that all employees participating in the preparation and service of the final product should share in whatever gratuitous rewards were being offered by customers, rather than splitting the reward only among those employees who had direct contact with the customers. Then again, we have learned that the inclusive or mandatory tipping system was implemented in the European countries because the travelers at that time did not understand the money exchanges and the customs, so tips were added onto the bill to assure that service people would not be cheated out of their fair returns for the services they performed. However, it was also noted that it became necessary to tip beyond the added service charges to be assured of any service at all. This is still the practice in many foreign countries.

By including the service charges (usually 10-15%) employers were able to redistribute this sum to the employees, including some workers like dishwashers, public relations people and busboys whose job function was not classified as production or service, but had some supportive role in the proper execution of the production and service functions. The additional charge was labeled "Service Comparis" and carefully included in the price of the meal, which meant that although the customer was aware of the service charge, it did not stick out on the bottom of the guest check like a penalty for having dined there.

Although the inclusive system is not prevalent throughout the United States or the Communist countries, a few restaurants, hotels, resorts and private clubs do practice this custom. However, when this is the practice, it is necessary that the public be informed in the menus or advertisements.

Advance Tipping

Another practice of prearranged gratuities is that the tip be contracted for in advance. This is primarily for large parties, conventions, catering, cruises and travel. The add-on gratuities are figured in many ways, but mostly on a percentage basis. Besides being used to fairly distribute the tip, add-on gratuities are sometimes used to subsidize labor costs or to cover any shortages. Add-on gratuities do not necessarily guarantee better service, as substantiated by our Tippers International surveys.

Advance payment for service is generally contrary to the rules of tipping. An evaluation procedure should take place to determine the amount of a tip, and if the service has not yet been performed, there is really nothing to evaluate. Generally, it is impossible, therefore, to tip properly in advance.

Some people misuse the concept of tipping to take advantage of others. Many feel we are stretching a point, but few realize that their payment of an advance so-called tip actually takes them into the realm of bribery. The person slips a few dollars to the hostess or maitre d' for a special table, which has not been reserved in advance, denies other people who are waiting their right to be treated fairly. An honest serving person will not accept such a payment and a thinking patron will not ask for the favor since it will surely backfire in the future. A maitre d' or hostess who accepts a bribe from you will accept one from someone else another time and it could escalate to a contest between the highest bidders. This has nothing to do with gratuities in the context of tipping. If special seating is provided without advance payment then the favor becomes a part of the service to be evaluated. Payment of a tip after the service is given is, in fact, a justifiable reward.

There are exceptions to the "never tip in advance" rule. Banquet and meeting planners who feed and serve groups of people make a common practice of adding and quoting gratuity service charges in advance usually on a percentage basis. Generally, these are not paid in advance, giving the person paying the bill an opportunity to take exception to the gratuity charge later, if the service has not been up to the agreed upon standards.

Often tips are paid for information which cannot be verified until later. For example, you may ask a doorman for directions. You tip him when he gives you the information, not after you return. Even though the doorman did provide the information, there is not a guarantee that the information is valid and therefore the giving of a tip might be considered an advance payment. But, in some situations, you simply tip and take a chance.

There are also occasions when it is wise to pay at least part of an intended tip in advance to insure that a task is remembered and carried out. An example would be if you are attending the theatre, and are expecting an urgent message. If you notify the management or usher and request special arrangements so that the message will reach you, it is justifiable to pay at least a portion of the tip in advance, to assure that your request will be carried out and not forgotten.

Tipping in advance for favors has been used throughout the world and no doubt will continue in the future. We find this to be true more so in larger cities, resort areas and popular vacation spots where more entertainment is provided.

Arriving at a place like Las Vegas for the first time can be mystifying. And dealing with fine, multi-star restaurants in cities like San Francisco can also be a puzzle. Such places have well defined rules about advance and add-on gratuities. If these are explained in the advertising and on the menus, you must abide by these policies. But, if advance tipping is not listed or advertised, you have the right to dispute it.

You can be caught up in a series of add-on gratuities without knowing about it. Add-on tips can be as high as 50%, particularly for dinner theatres where the tickets for the play include the price of the dinner. It is always advisable to check the terms of the ticket when you make the purchase.

Add-on tips can be equally confusing for bus tours, plane and rail travel, cruises, scheduled group tours and vacations. Be sure to examine all policies because additional charges could increase the cost of the trip and greatly inhibit your spending power while you are traveling.

Free Tipping

The free tipping system refers to the optional choice of the individual to bestow money, gifts or other types of favors as a reward for service well done. This concept embraces the idea that tipping should be left up to the individual. After all, tipping should be voluntary and tipping that is paid out involuntarily should not be considered tipping. Proponents of the free tipping concept suggest that everyone should be entitled to withhold a tip even in situations where tipping is customary, just as one should feel free to offer a tip where none is expected or required.

In the free tipping system the tips are sometimes divided and shared with other workers the same as with those working under the inclusive or mandatory system. But, the division of these tips varies according to agreement or policy of the establishment. Some pool their tips and divide them equally. However, this sometimes causes problems among the workers because the poorer performing or lazy ones share with the more competent workers. After a while this conflict of feeling can surface in the type of service performed; and not only do the service people suffer, but management also feels the pinch resulting from loss of business. If there is a division of tips among the workers it should be handled according to the established policies.

In years past we found that people who worked in the service trades were satisfied with an average of ten percent of the bill. Ten percent seemed to be the standard for tipping waiters, waitresses, bellboys, the porter and the shoeshine boy. The situation today has changed not only in the percentage of the tip, but also in the fact that there are more people providing services, and because of our ever-increasing travel and entertaining. Inflation has affected the cost of everything, including the rise in tip percentage from 10% to 15%. In vacation and resort areas and posh establishments, the tips have even increased to an expected 20% and higher.

If some control isn't initiated or guidelines established, the whole concept of tipping will destroy itself or we could wind up with some kind of controls that will take away our freedom of choice to reward for services received. Not only will the public lose their freedom of expression, but management could lose their method of subsidizing labor costs through the free tipping system. Workers might also be limited as to what they can expect as gratuity for their services. This could put management into a position that all their service people would work on a percentage of the establishment's gross income or be on a commission basis, which would destroy the incentive of giving good service.

Special gifts are also creeping into the giving of gratuities. Service people often look for incentives on holidays, their birthdays, and before their vacations. Most of these special gifts are in lieu of normal tips and gratuities. Some are given in advance for future service and some are given as an expression of extra appreciation. When these get out of hand, the customer could find himself with an obligation far beyond the norm. On the other hand, the service person can work this gift giving to an extreme by suggesting what they would like to receive. Giving a gift as an incentive for future service, or as a tip for service already received should be done carefully after much evaluation of the individual situation.

CHAPTER 4

***

Evaluating Service/Tipping Formulas

"What You Receive is What You Leave" is the Tippers International slogan. We should always remember that a tip is not an obligation and that the tip should always be left up to the discretion of the consumer. The consumer, according to their own standards, should evaluate the service received and choose to leave a tip or not leave a tip. You shouldn't ever have to feel obligated in any way because of this decision.

Expect Professional Service

When the consumer enters into a place of business, he expects to be waited on in a professional manner. It is the same as if you were hiring someone to work for you and serve you the product you are buying. In the case of the hospitality industry we find that most of the services received are in hotels, restaurants, motels, and taxis and other modes of transportation. There are many services that we as consumers cannot provide for ourselves any more. We have to rely on travel agents to make our travel reservations, service people to repair our appliances and cars, nursing home attendants to care for our elderly, garbage men to collect our refuse, beauticians and barbers to do our hair, and mailmen, newspaper boys and deliverymen to bring our mail, papers and packages. The list continues to grow, the world is growing smaller, and greater numbers of people are on the move. In order to cope with this ever increasing problem, we have to rely on others for services, and for this we compensate the service people with tips and gratuities as well as wages.

Always remember that you should never tip for future service or tip for the back of the house, the people who indirectly affect the service you receive. Always tip the contact person for the type and style of service which makes your stay or visit pleasant. Also, a tip should always be accompanied by a smile and a thank you.

Times are changing and we must change with them. You will find that there are more places to leave tips than ever before and each year we find new services with which to deal. Older people and seasoned travelers have been able to cope with these new services because they have come gradually. But, each new generation entering into the business world can be lost as to what to do in unfamiliar places and situations.

Those who enter into the service field are going into a field of employment that is growing fast and is becoming very lucrative. It is a field where a person can assert professionalism and gain status by using their abilities to serve other people for profit. This field does not take any initial financial investment, and an individual can choose their own place to work. Some choose smaller establishments while others choose large operations, but both offer opportunities to exercise ability to achieve success in the service field. It is also a profession which can be entered without advanced schooling. There are many vocational and technical schools that offer specialized courses for students training to be professional service people. Often, places of employment will also teach a person professional service skills according to policies of the establishments.

These educational opportunities for service people afford many the chance to earn a substantial income. Their only cost is measured in the hours they spend working and learning. Being in the service trades or the hospitality industry is an honorable profession and we recognize that our society cannot survive without these capable service people.

Tipping Judgements

We also find that when the service people become the consumers, they are more critical toward receiving services than

34

an ordinary consumer. If they are professional and successful in their own position, they also expect to be treated as they treat others. This is good for the free enterprise system in which tipping and gratuities play such an important part. The tipping system has existed without any government regulations, because people feel free to compensate others for services they cannot or choose not to do for themselves. These are services that make life easier, more pleasant and rewarding.

Some people dislike tipping and do not tip or tip very little. They feel that the employer has an obligation to serve the customers without having to subsidize the labor costs through tips. This is perfectly legal and there is no obligation for anyone to leave a tip for any kind of service if they do not wish to. However, some people, through their shortcomings and obsessions against tipping, will leave a penny or small coin. This is really an insult to the service person and it would be better not to leave anything. At least then the service person might think that the customer forgot, does not believe in tipping, or possibly cannot afford to tip.

We know that all service is not equal, so you must evaluate each person carefully, and evaluate the circumstances under which they are working. A busy day or night might make a professional seem inadequate and it is possible that you could help make their day if you can allow them to relax while you are being served. Service people working in the hospitality trades are an absolute necessity, so it is important that consumers encourage these people to perform well.

Expansion of Service Industry

With the population increasing, and people living longer, each year we find that more and more people are entering into the service field. More service people are needed to care for the growing numbers of elderly. More service people are required to maintain and repair our increasing number of appliances, computers and machines. Robots are being introduced in almost every field and more service people will be required to keep them in working order. New modes of transportation for travel and business will require more service people to handle the increased numbers of people on the move. Women entering the work force will require more services and facilities to handle their requirements in hotels, motels and transportation.

The job market is changing from outmoded manufacturing to more high-technology industries which will employ many more service people. This will create new jobs, not only in new industry, but will also provide opportunities to service existing technical equipment now being installed throughout organizations worldwide.

We find that there are more white-collar workers compared to blue collar workers by at least 10%. This will take in new services in many fields and some of these will affect the tipping process and increase the number of services with which we will all have to cope. Through technological evolution, we've become an information society. At the present time, 5 out of 10 jobs are information jobs. And in the next 20 years, 7 out of 10 jobs will fall into the information category.

According to the U.S. Census Bureau in the year 2000, the population of 16 year olds and over was just over 209,000,000. About 70,000,000 were not in the labor force. About 19,000,000 were employed in service occupations. The total population of the U.S. at the same time was 281,000,000 with 6,000,000 more females than males with the median age being 35 years.

The Bureau of Labor Statistics reported that over 10,000,000 people were employed in the food preparation and serving industry. This would place this industry as being the third largest in U.S., only being surpassed by sales, office and administrative, and employing just slightly over what the production industry does.

The food preparation serving industry is the lowest paying with an average yearly income of $17,400.00. It is no wonder why tipping is necessary. The lowest paying occupation was fast food cook who averaged $7.28 per hour. Five of the six lowest paying occupations were related to food preparation and serving.

There are over 2,000,000 waiters and waitresses and over 2,000,000 workers in the combined food preparation and serving workers, including fast food. About 66% of these workers are paid less than $8.50 per hour.

Listed in our table are the average wages of the various positions in the food preparation and serving related occupations.

	Per Hour
Chefs and head cooks	$16.00
First-line supervisors/managers of food preparation and serving workers	$13.03
Cooks, fast food	$7.28
Cooks, institution and cafeteria	$9.42
Cooks, restaurant	$9.68
Cooks, short order	$8.39
Food preparation workers	$8.43
Bartenders	$8.15
Combined food preparation and serving workers, including fast food	$7.36
Counter attendants, cafeteria, food concession and coffee shop	$7.79
Waiters and waitresses	$7.63
Food servers, non restaurant	$8.44
Dining room, cafeteria attendants and Bartender's helpers	$7.41
Dishwashers	$7.47
Host and Hostesses, restaurant, lounge and coffee shop	$7.79

In the year 2002, there were 144,000,000 people employed in 10 different occupations. Over 26,000,000 were employed in service occupations which ranked second only to professional and related occupations. This was approximately 18.4% of distribution and is expected to grow. The tipping process will be affected especially if the rates stay low. This will take in new services in many fields and some of these will definitely affect the over-all tipping process and increase the number of services with which we will all have to cope.

It is also predicted that the growth in the service sector and within the 35-45 year old age range, which is considered the high earning period of people's lives, there are approximately 12,000,000 families, each with two adults working full-time. Over the next decade this group is expected to increase by 50%. They will have to depend on others to provide basic services. So, we can look forward to a great growth in the service field.

And as we look forward to an increase in life expectancy, the need for jobs and services for the elderly will also increase.

In years to come, people will be working shorter hours and will have more leisure time to expend on travel, dining and entertainment — all which will increase the number of service people needed in the hospitality industry — from the smallest establishments all the way up to the giant hotel and motel chains.

We anticipate that a lot more of the people will be entering the service trades to provide services for the general public, services that we as consumers cannot do without. We are becoming more dependent on outside services in this ever-changing world and it is time that we set some standards and rules to follow so that we can all share the freedom of expression by rewarding others according to our own standards for services that help make life more pleasant when away from home. We should respect the professionalism of service people and they, in turn, should respect the consumer.

There are, however, those who are not tipped. In some cases, signs will announce rules against tipping. If you are uncertain about the tipping policy in a certain situation, ask management personnel for guidance.

As we mentioned in our book, airline attendants are not tipped even though their counterparts on ships and trains generally are. It's an especially interesting phenomenon in light of the fact that air travel is the most recent form of transportation to evolve in a world where tipping seems to be gaining an ever stronger foothold. The airline attendant's job has always been thought of as offering other benefits in addition to wages, such as glamorous and inexpensive travel to exciting lands.

Service station attendants, except those who perform an extraordinary service, are also among the ranks of non-tippees. But with the increasing popularity of self-service stations and the diminishing number of stations which put gas in your tank, clean your windows, check your oil and put air in your tires, their numbers are being severely diminished. Maybe we'll have to start tipping to bring back those convenient days.

Theater ushers are generally not tipped in this country, but be careful to check the local custom when you go over-seas. In many countries, you will have to be prepared to fumble in the dark for an exact coin before taking your seat.

Don't tip the owner of a beauty parlor. The idea is that he or she is an entrepreneur and can make it on her or his own without gratuities like other business owners.

You're under no obligation to tip car or rental agents, airport coach drivers or employees of the airlines who take in your baggage at the arrival area. Their employers are generally compensating them for the service, which we understand is appropriate.

Professional tennis instructors, camp counselors and similar employees in recreation-oriented fields, in most cases, are not allowed to accept tips or do not expect to receive gratuities. However, there are people that might make an offer.

No tips to bankers, stock brokers, real estate people or insurance men. This might be considered as some form of bribery and is kind of an endangered action. Nor do you tip those store clerks who help you with your purchases, though there was a time in U.S. cities when they were widely tipped.

FORMULAS

This brings us to the question of which system should be used to determine the size of the tip given to the service professional. The most common systems will be discussed here, although there are probably almost as many systems as there are people — each of us with our own styles and adjustments. As we've mentioned, tipping is a free enterprise system and there should be a complete freedom of choice as to how much to tip. The following systems are presented as helpful guides.

Percentage System

The majority of tippers choose a percentage of the bill to determine the amount of tip. Percentages should be used only in situations where a specific price is given for goods or services. Years ago, the norm was 10% or 10 cents for every dollar. At that time there were only a few people to tip, including waiters and waitresses, porters, bellboys and the shoeshine boys.

Porters made a living on their tips, but all they had to offer was their services. Waiters in railway dining cars were tipped for their services, as were the porters. But, the shoeshine boy performed a service and furnished the material for his work. So what he charged for his service was not all profit. He had to pay rent for his space and buy his shoe polish. If the stand was in the barber shop, he generally had to split his take with the owner. If his stand was in a railroad station or another place of business, he had to pay some amount for rent. The tip was based on his charge and sometimes went beyond the normal 10% depending on the type of service he provided. For example, when a shine was 50 cents and he got a dime tip, he was on a 20% tipping schedule, or twice the normal amount. As the price went up, the tip increased. The same happens today with food, lodging, travel and other types of service.

In the last few years the percentage of tipping has increased from 15% to as high as 20%. Even so, some service people are not satisfied and want 20-25%. Through the years of following this pattern, we have not been able to determine actually who, why or how the percentage became 15% and more. If, as the price of food, lodging and travel increased, the tipping rate had stayed at 10%, the amount of money tipped would still have increased with the price of the product. But now everyone wants an average of 15%, even though the service they provide is sometimes inferior. This is what causes consumers to feel that they are being exploited and yet they feel obligated to leave a tip in spite of the service they receive.

On the other hand, if we look at the problem from the service person's standpoint we might find an altogether different angle. Most service people are quite professional, especially if they work in a reputable place of business that uses the tipping method to subsidize their labor costs. They have to be able to do their job in an efficient manner, be courteous, pleasant, clean, and carry on the goodwill of the business because they are the direct contact with the customer. Even the most professional service people sometimes find it difficult to deal with all customers in the same efficient manner, because all customers are not alike. Some demand more service than others and their value of good service may differ from time to time. Some people will never be satisfied no matter how well they are treated. But, this is the nature of this type of work and service people must be able to take the bad with the good. When problems do arise, the truly professional service person will take whatever tip is given, go cheerfully to the next customer and continue to provide the best service possible.

But, how do you determine the percentage to be used to figure the tip?

What You Receive Is What You Leave Formula

One of the objections you may have to using the percentage formula in food service establishments may result from the variety of services that are provided. The customary rate of 15% cannot be applied everywhere because services offered are not standardized. If you remember the formula — "What You Receive, Is What You Leave," and immediately ask yourself who is doing the work, your eyes will be opened and the answers will be clear to you.

Simply reduce the percentage according to the reductions in services. Let's take a quick look at the basic service functions provided in restaurants where 15% tips are applicable:

1. seating is provided or arranged for you
2. a place is set for you
3. your order is taken at your seat

4. food and drink are served at your seat
5. extra service is offered while you eat
6. your check is delivered to you

When these basic services are provided, the full 15% tip is appropriate for timely, efficient, and courteous performance.

Cafeterias are another matter because they provide fewer services. Seating is provided, but you do nearly everything else yourself. You pick up your own flatware and table setting, place your own order, carry your own food, return to the serving line for refills or condiments, and take the check to the cashier, or pay at the end of the line before you have had one bite. Since you perform most of the basic tasks, obviously no tipping is expected in such establishments. However, a tip of 5% might be appreciated especially if you visit the restaurant quite often.

Fast food restaurants, on the other hand, are often misunderstood. Places falling into the fast food category often provide all six basic  services listed above and thereby qualify for the full 15% gratuity. People sometimes consider multi-unit restaurant operations or chains to be in the jiffy food category, but this is far from the truth. Actually, some of the best run dining operations in the United States are part of chain operations. Never assume because a restaurant is part of a franchise system that it automatically falls under a no tip plan.

Truck stops, diners and lunch counters can also be misinterpreted when it comes to tipping. The food may be simple and the surroundings ordinary in these establishments, but the service people usually perform the same tasks for you as waiters in fancier places; and they sometimes work harder for less money. These individuals deserve the full 15% tip for their efforts.

At the opposite end of the food services spectrum are the gourmet and formal dining establishments where a wider range of services are provided. Extra courses are served, and trained specialists perform duties tailored to more refined dining experiences. It may take hours to fully enjoy your dining. Needless to say, these extras may account for gratuities up to 30%, depending on what you receive and how it is delivered.

The six basic services listed above, even if provided by one person, make tipping up to 15% appropriate. More services, such as a wine steward, a table steward, and special courtesies from the captain, should be rewarded as you consider them appropriate.

In general, add a five percent tip for every two services provided. If four services are delivered, leave a 10% tip, and additional ones beyond the six listed should raise it above the standard 15%. In the more exclusive eating establishments, it may be appropriate to raise the tip from five percent for every two services to a larger percent or to pay an extra percentage for the extra services.

Ten Plus or Minus Five Formula

The most commonly used formula to figure percentages simply is the 10% plus or minus five percent formula. This formula is designed for quite general use to speed up the tipping process which can be dragged on by hair splitting. It is a simple formula to apply. First look at the price and determine 10% by mentally moving the decimal point one digit to the left. To arrive at the additional five percent, determine half of your 10% amount. Add the 10% and five percent figures and you've got your 15% tip! Double your 10% answer for a 20% tip.

To use an evaluation system with this formula, simply decide whether the service was good, fair or poor. These three categories apply to the rates of 15, 10 or five percent. If you feel the service is worse than five percent, leave no tip at all. If the service was exceptional or if extra courses were served, as in some of the more exclusive restaurants, tip 20% or more, as you feel appropriate.

One for Seven Formula

This approach is not as accurate as the one above, but it is nonetheless acceptable. It is done by dividing the total amount of the bill by seven. For example, if the price is $35.00, the tip would be five dollars. When you divide the billed amount by seven, your answer is a little more than 14% or just short of the customary 15%. You might add a small amount if you wish to follow the 15%

for good service rule. For the $35.00 example given, another 25 cents would bring the tip up to the full 15% amount. Remember, when you use this formula, you must be satisfied with the service or your reward will be too generous.

Times Sales Tax Formula

Some people use the sales tax as a base for figuring tips. This formula can be less accurate than the others, but it keeps you in the ballpark. Be careful when applying this formula because it can trip you up in some cases, especially if you are in a state where you are not familiar with the local sales tax rate. If the state were you receive the services levies a five percent sales tax and you wish to tip the customary 15%, simply multiply the amount of tax shown on the bill by three. If the service was only fair, multiply by two to figure a 10% tip, and for exceptional service, multiply by four to arrive at a 20% tip.

The tax structure in some states is not always that easy for helping determine tips. Some charge eight percent and others four percent, and the multiplication problems can become more complex. But, however you multiply, the object is to come as close to the percent you wish to leave and then round it off as you see fit.

Rounding Up and Rounding Down

When you use one of the four suggested formulas and the evaluation scale of good, fair or poor service, you will frequently find the need for rounding off amounts. Rounding off has an advantage in that it offers you an extra means of expression. A good rule to follow is to round up to give the server the benefit of a doubt, or round down to give an extra edge to a smaller tip. Some tippers prefer to round up or down in quarters or half dollar amounts, while others even prefer nickels and dimes for ultimate accuracy. There is no set rule, be as exact as you wish.

Flat Tip System

Some people use a flat method for tipping. They will leave even money without trying to figure a percentage. If the service and product are satisfactory their flat tip is sufficient in their opinion, and this is what makes this free enterprise system so successful — because all tips should be based on service, not just percentages. As we have said so many times before, service is one of the oldest acts of hospitality in existence. The person who selects the flat tip system believes that the service should be analyzed solely on the service and not the price of the product. After all, say the advocates of flat tipping, it takes no more service to serve a prime rib dinner than it does to serve a chicken dinner, but the final bill will be considerably different, and therefore the tip, based on the percentage system, would also be considerably different.

Some waiters and other tippees also disagree with percentage rates because of the inequities in restaurants. Serving people often wish flat fees were possible to help them realize a predictable return for their work in restaurants where seating is limited. One guest occupying a seat for an hour during a noon lunch period may spend five dollars, while another occupying a seat for the same hour may spend $15.00. The difference in tip revenue is obvious. One guest may leave a 75 cent tip while the other tips $2.25. If the waiter serves 20 such seats, the revenue for that hour (depending on the size of the checks) could vary from $15.00 to $45.00 if the percentage system is used.

In spite of such inequities, there is no movement among tippees and tippers to stop using percentages. People seem more content with a system that they understand than to go through the process of reeducating the public about tipping. Furthermore, public acceptance of a new system would be difficult to achieve. So, it seems that the percentage system will continue to be used in those situations where a specific price for goods or services is charged. However, in cases where a specific price is not given, the flat tip system should be used according to the guidelines set forth in the next chapters.

PART II
Who, Where
&
How Much

CHAPTER 5

***

Restaurants And Nightclubs

Tipping is a universal language in itself, because we all use tipping to communicate our degree of satisfaction for services we receive. Tipping has become a tool that everyone understands. It is used in various forms as compensation for services that we often cannot provide for ourselves. Tipping standards have become established in most places, however there are exceptions where tipping is not accepted as a general rule.

Tipping purists will adhere reasonably well to those standards that assure that consumers, serving professionals and service management are all thinking and speaking in the same language. The following standard tipping amounts are set forth to establish and promote satisfactory service and to identify you as a respected and understanding tipper.

Our specific situations tell who, where, when and how much to tip. They are arranged by serving trade classification for easier reference. Wherever possible we have included the "why" of each tipping situation to add perspective and also to demonstrate how the rules of tipping actually apply. The following are serving persons you may encounter in full service restaurants — from the parking lot attendant to the cashier. All situations assume that the service you receive is completely satisfactory.

Parking Lot Attendant

*Tip $1.00 to $2.00
when your car is delivered.*

If your car is parked for you and delivered to you, tip $2.00. If it is parked for you or retrieved, not both, a $1.00 tip is adequate. If the restaurant charges a parking fee, you are not expected to tip the person who delivers your car. Do not tip a parking booth attendant unless some special security or other service was provided for you while parked.

When a restaurant invests in space for free customer parking, it is a gesture of consideration for the customers. If the free parking convenience is embellished by staff parking attendants, it is clearly in your interest to augment their often less than minimum wage by tipping to help the restaurant maintain the service. If, however, the restaurant runs the lot like a business, charging a parking fee, you may assume it is either on a self-paying or profit making basis and no tip is needed.

Doorman

Tip only for special service.

No tip is expected if no service is given beyond the routine opening of doors. If help is given in unloading equipment for meetings and such, you may tip two to three dollars, depending on the value of the service to you. If you have the doorman order your car in advance, so that it's waiting for you, send a dollar tip via the waiter or cashier with your request. Be sure to specify to whom the tip should go. For ultimate service, such as asking as you enter to have your car at the door at a specified departure time, you may tip as much as two dollars to the doorman who makes the arrangements.

Doormen serve two or three valuable functions for management. They help control automobile traffic, provide watchful security to avoid insurance claims and they have a definite value as colorful window dressing. They usually receive reasonable wages for their time without the need for tip revenue to make a living.

Cloakroom Attendant

Tip 50¢ to $1.00 per garment.

Tip 50 cents to $1.00 for each coat, but not extra for hats or parcels unless you have several items or they are large and bulky requiring extra space. In that case, tip 50 cents extra. Remember that you are paying for security as well as convenience. If the cloakroom is not well watched and not closed to general public access, adjust your tip accordingly.

The hospitality industry could make improvements in this phase of their operation. Clothes are becoming more and more expensive and we know that women, in particular, are often afraid to leave their personal belongings in a cloakroom that is not watched. This indecision places them in an upsetting and frustrating position and they cannot enjoy their luncheon or evening out. We feel that it is the hospitality industry's responsibility to assure the safety of the personal belongings of their valued customers. This necessary service could be handled in different ways. The restaurants could set up outside sources to handle their cloakrooms or allow handicapped persons a chance to operate them and become productive.

Restroom Attendant

Tip 25¢ to $1.00

If the restroom is clean and a towel is offered, a small tip of 50 cents, but no more than $1.00 is in order. If no service is provided, no tip is required. It is impossible to prepare for all tipping situations and in a case like this, you might give only what is loose in your pocket.

Host or Hostess

No tip for handling routine reservations and seating.

If special service is provided, such as extra efforts to make unexpected or unusual table arrangements for guests in your group, or for arranging a table in a particular location, feel free to discreetly tip up to $5.00.

Pay it directly to the host or hostess who makes the special effort. A good host or hostess is a highly qualified, often diplomatic person and usually salaried at more than waiters and waitresses. He or she performs a vitally important service for management, regulating the flow of customers to various seating areas, preventing overloading of serving people, enhancing service to customers and giving all serving people a fair and equal chance for tip income. These people often share in the total tip revenue in places using the tipping pool system. Also, keep in mind that slipping them a five or ten dollar bill to be seated ahead of others who may even have reservations when you do not, is bribery, not tipping, and does no credit to either of you.

Maitre d' hotel

No tip unless you request or receive special service.

Tip the maitre d' only for special services or favors such as making special arrangements with the chef and serving staff for birthday or anniversary observances, or for handling and coordinating with the staff unusual seating arrangements which may require a management policy decision. Tip discreetly and directly to the maitre d' from five to ten dollars depending on the difficulty or irregularity of your request and whether it must be accomplished under crowded conditions. This also may depend on your availability of cash and your budget.

Remember that the maitre d'hotel is a management person salaried as a right arm of ownership. As often as not, tips offered by a customer are accepted only to avoid offending the customer. If you do tip, make sure you do it tastefully. Don't be surprised if the tip is declined. If you are a regular customer, you may find a small personal or unusual gift from time to time will be just as expensive and more effective.

Headwaiter

No tip unless you receive special service.

If the headwaiter provides special service, such as making special arrangements with the chef or a waiter, add three to five percent to the final percent you tip for the meal. The headwaiter usually shares in the tipping pool, or shares directly with the waiter or waitress. Remember the "What You Receive is What You Leave" formula. Those people who provide you extra service are worth the additional tip.

Captain

No tip unless special service is received.

The captain is in charge of all waiters and waitresses in one section of a large restaurant. In a smaller restaurant you may not have a captain, but a headwaiter who is in charge of all waiters and waitresses in the entire restaurant. If he makes special arrangements for you with the chef, cooks at your tableside, bones the seafood, prepares the dressings and so forth, tip as you would a headwaiter. Add three to five percent extra when you figure your final tip for the meal.

Captains and headwaiters often share in the tipping pool or work directly with waiters and waitresses to receive a share of their tips. Adding a three to five percent amount to the percent you tip will reward both the captain or headwaiter, and your waiter or waitress when they share the tip.

Wine Steward

Tip 10% to 15% of the cost of the wine you purchase.

Take pains to notice whether the restaurant you are patronizing really has a wine steward. Often you will find that restaurants with a casual attitude will simply accommodate their customers by giving the job of taking your wine order to the captain or headwaiter. If the restaurant has no special wine steward, instead of tipping 10-15% of the wine bill, simply tip as you would for a headwaiter's or captain's service at your table. Add three to five percent to the final percent you tip.

Wine is an extra purchase which, to be enjoyed to its fullest, should be ordered with as much care as the courses of your meal. For this level of enjoyment a true wine steward is needed, someone who has done considerable specialized preparation. The wine steward should be familiar with all the establishment's wines and adept at describing them to help you understand whether or not you would like them. This task should be performed without pretense, yet with flair and bearing.

It is entirely possible that a captain or headwaiter could still perform as a qualified wine steward. If this is the case, then tip equally well (10-15%).

A good wine steward is worth 15% of the wine bill. Try to tip them in person at the time you leave. Customarily, the wine steward will be available near your table or the cashier's post as you leave, or will find another convenient opportunity to receive the tip. If the wine steward is otherwise occupied, put the tip in an envelope and leave it with the cashier or waiter with instructions to relay it to the wine steward.

A wine steward who does little more than read the wine list and take your order is worth less, regardless of how well the wine is served. Tip only 10% in this case if the person appears to lack knowledge or interest.

Waiter or Waitress

Tip 15% in restaurants providing all six basic services.

The six basic services to consider when determining your tip are:
1. seating is provided or arranged for you;
2. a place is set for you;
3. your order is taken at your seat;
4. food and drink are served at your seat;
5. extra service is offered while you eat;
6. your check is delivered to you.

If these six basic services are provided in a professional and satisfactory manner, then your waiter or waitress has earned a 15% tip. If this is one of the finer restaurants or night clubs and the service is excellent, a tip of 20% or more is in order.

Lunch Counter Personnel

Tip based on what you eat.

Lunch counter service is considered quick or fast service and is not considered the same as a full service meal. Ten percent of the total bill is the norm, but if the bill is small, still leave at least 15 cents. No tip is necessary for coffee or drink without food.

Buffets, Smorgasbords,
Truck Stops and Cafeterias

Tip based on service received.

In these places where full service is not provided and you serve yourself, it is not necessary to tip the same as a full service place of business. If the server does no more than bring water or serve coffee or remove plates, it is not necessary to tip over 10% of the bill. If less is provided, no tip, or a token of five percent of the total bill, can be left.

Busboy

No tips.

Busboys are paid a regular hourly wage for their work and should not be tipped. Many restaurants which use the tipping pool system ask their waiters and waitresses to share a few percent with the busboys. Where tips are not pooled, waiters and waitresses often make individual deals with busboys to enlist their cooperation.

Bartender

10% to 15% of the bar bill,
when you leave the bar.

One person ordering one drink should tip a minimum of 50 cents. If you pay each time you are served a drink at the bar, a 10% tip is correct. If the bartender keeps a bar tab for you, or if you pay by credit card, tip 15% for the extra work it takes.

If you are a regular customer and your bartender remembers what you drink, knows how you like to pay and gives you valued customer treatment, tip 15% anyway.

Often special services are required, such as bringing you a telephone at the bar, relaying messages for you or keeping you posted on information that will interest you. These situations warrant an extra five percent, or perhaps a special gift of personal interest.

Cocktail Waitress

10% tip when you pay as served.

Extra work deserves extra gratuities. If the cocktail waitress keeps a bar tab for you, transfers your bar check to the waiter or waitress in the dining room, prepares credit card papers or serves hors d'oeuvres or snacks with the drinks, tip 15%. Paying drink by drink, as served, with none of the above extras is less work and only worth 10%.

Musicians

*Tip $1 to $5 for
requests you make.*

Tip one dollar per request from strolling players. Tip one dollar per request at piano bars, but up to two dollars if the pianist plays two or three requests in half an hour to a full hour period. If the pianist makes you the star of a sing-along, consider asking the pianist to join you in a cocktail. If you spend two hours or more, you should consider tipping as much as three dollars when you leave.

Tip two to three dollars per request to a small orchestra or combo. Since there are several musicians involved, the amount should be worth sharing. Larger groups and bands should receive up to five dollars for the same reason.

CHAPTER 6
***

Hotels, Motels
& Resorts

The public and service industry must realize that in this country there are different wage scales throughout the country and various classes of people. Many people are not aware of proper tipping or can't afford what might be recommended. Some people might plan and save all year for their yearly vacation and then find there might not be enough cash for proper tipping. In our book we try to make a large enough selection of recommendations on tipping to include everyone.

When people travel, whether for business or pleasure, they feel comfortable in certain surroundings and they are used to having certain personal belongings with them. Famed stand-up comedian George Carlin is well known for his referral to "people and their stuff." Wherever people go they have certain "stuff" they have to take with them or "stuff" they need when they get where they are going. It's no problem when you are at home where your "stuff" is, but when you travel and are surrounded by the unfamiliar, it helps to have people who are familiar with where to get the things you need and to handle the "stuff" you have to take with you from place to place. This necessity of travel life gave birth to the many serving professions in the hospitality industry. These service people anticipate what things you will need, where you have to go, how to get you there and how to help you remove some of the natural strain of the mobile life. These usually outgoing, hard working professionals, who are often worth their weight in gold, make themselves available for a lot less than gold, thanks to the tipping merit pay system.

Hospitality industry serving people, unlike their food service industry counterparts, work primarily on the basis of a flat fee as opposed to a percentage of a specific purchase price. Here in the world of travel the serious tipper will take pains to be aware of who gets how much for what.

Hotel/Motel Doorman

No tip for routine door opening.
Whistling for a cab, $1.00 to $2.00
Tip $1 to $5.00 for other services.

 Tip the doorman 50 cents to $1.00 for any of these individual aids: if he provides non-hotel information you request, helps you unload or load your car, provides an umbrella for members of your party, phones for a taxi when one is not nearby, arranges your parking, calls for your car, summons a porter or bellboy, watches your car at streetside while you do business inside (if excessive time, tip one dollar) or provides special help in any way.

Tip up to two dollars when he performs any two of these services, but don't automatically increase the tip by 50 cents for every additional one. Normally a one dollar tip covers whatever needs to be done. Consider increasing the tip, however, for extra thoughtfulness, such as having your car waiting when you phone order it ahead, locking it or taking other security measures or taking extra time to get information or arrange services for you.

It is amazing how tipping the doorman one dollar can ease the awkwardness of getting your "stuff" in or out of a hotel or motel.

For longer stays, a $15.00 tip when you arrive or a couple of dollars twice a week will assure you of a watchful and helpful friend at the door. Don't expect too much, however, and remember you have different doormen at different times. Your man cannot be there 24 hours a day.

Parking Attendant

Tip $1.00 for delivering your car.
More in very large hotels.

Do not tip the parking booth attendant when you park and pick up your own car.

One dollar is adequate in hotels and motels with up to 100 rooms, but consider tipping up to two dollars in large hotels where the logistics of stacking several hundred autos increases the length of time it takes an attendant to physically reach and retrieve your car.   Time, however, is not always a good gauge of how far away your car may be parked.   Sometimes it can be a measure of dawdling or confusion.   You be the judge.   Watch the bearing of the attendant.   See how he handles your car.

Bellboy

Tip 50¢ to $1.00 per suitcase or bag.
50¢ for small cases.
Extra for very awkward bags or trunks.

Extenuating circumstances could modify this guideline for tipping the bellboy and the tip should be based on time and effort. If the bellboy does more than escort you and your luggage from the lobby to your room consider increasing the tip.   For example, if the bellboy meets you at your car to load your luggage onto a cart, waits while you check in at the desk, then escorts you to the room and places your luggage on racks and hangs your garment bags, reward the bellboy for the extra time and effort.

A bellboy is an excellent source of information, too.   Since you spend a few moments with the bellboy enroute to your room, the opportunity is there to tap his knowledge about things you will need or places you want to go.   Good information is another consideration when you decide how much to tip.

Apply the guideline given in the heading for baggage handling and then consider the extra time, effort and information given. A good tip upon arrival wins you a willing worker during your stay. Also, remember that if you have only one bag and it is carried to the farthest room in a large hotel, the 50 cents to $1.00 per bag guideline may not be enough.

Hotel Porter

Tip 50¢ to $1.00 except for specially ordered services.

Some hotels have a porter who helps unload or load your luggage and transport it to or from the desk.

The bellboy takes it from there. It would be unreasonable to expect you to pay a porter on the same scale as a bellboy because this would double the cost of getting in or out of a hotel lobby.

Specially ordered services, however, do warrant a bigger tip. If your family requires a special roll-away bed installed in your room or an extra table brought in, a porter is often summoned by the desk clerk or room service clerk to accomplish the task. Tip according to the extra time and effort required to get the equipment from a storeroom and install it in your room. Consider a one dollar tip in a case of this sort.

Porters may be called on to help carry materials or equipment to meeting rooms and conventions on the premises or help unload or load similar items in your car. Big jobs that take 15-30 minutes may be worth from two to three dollars — even more if the job is especially difficult or complex.

Desk Clerk

No tip unless special service is rendered.

A desk clerk is usually salaried the same as a hotel/motel cashier, and conducts routine business for management. No tip is required or expected for routine procedures.

There are some situations, however, for which a tip is appropriate. Consider tipping the desk clerk for services such as handling a specially large number of incoming or outgoing messages, holding packages at the desk for people, being especially efficient and careful in handling of valuables and carrying out other security favors for you. Base your tip on the value of the service to you and the manner in which it is done. One dollar is adequate for services one level above routine. Consider up to two dollars for special services a level higher.

If a desk clerk has helped you repeatedly over a stay of several days or weeks, it would be proper to consider a two up to five dollar tip before you leave if you have not tipped prior to leaving. Reward the desk clerk directly if possible, or leave the gratuity in an envelope bearing the clerk's name.

Switchboard Operator

No tips for routine services.

Telephone operators are salaried to carry out their duties in intra-hotel communication and no tip is expected.

There are times, however, when their help can be of great value. An example might be when you are leaving your room but wish incoming calls transferred to you in another suite or meeting place. Often an operator is happy to perform this service if you provide the information about where you wish the calls transferred. Often this can be done by calling the operator when leaving your room or stopping at the desk. If you ask for such special favors and plan to tip the operator (which is advised), be sure you get the operator's name. Later, after the service has been handled well, leave the tip in person or in an envelope with the operator's name on it.

Room Service Waiter

Never less than $1.00 or 15% of the bill,
whichever is higher.

Remember that a room service waiter not only has to transport items you need, but also has need for some of the skills of serving that you would expect from a waiter in a restaurant. There is no reason why they should not receive compensation at the same rate, if they are capable.

Tip more for special services such as opening champagne or pouring wine. Tip extra for these services even when the hotel charges corkage for guest supplied liquor.

Valet

No tip for work you deliver or
pick-up at the valet desk.

Tip $1.00 for delivery and/or pick-up at your room even though the cost may be added to your bill.

Tip extra when valet services must be obtained for you outside the hotel which requires a special trip for the valet. A one to two dollar tip is not unreasonable for outside valet service that takes 15 minutes or more to accomplish. Remember, the tip should be in addition to the price for the service.

Chambermaid

Tip $1.00 to $2.00 per night and
$5.00 to $10.00 per week.

These guidelines vary according to the quality of service and the facilities. Also take into consideration the amount of work done for you. If you have one room the above guideline is adequate. If you have two rooms or a suite of rooms consider tipping half again as much for quality service.

Take pains to insure that the maid will, in fact, receive the tip. Give it directly or leave it in an envelope in the room or at the desk bearing instructions "For the Maid — Room 111" so the chambermaid will be assured of receiving it and will know who left the tip.

Many people forget chambermaids when they do good work and tend to remember them only when there are no towels or soap.

Hospitality Desk Clerk

Tip only for free special services and special efforts on your behalf.

Do not tip for simple information on how to get somewhere, where a certain kind of store may be or information about the hotel/motel itself. Hospitality clerks, or hosts and hostesses, are salaried and provide an important function in relieving other personnel from having to take time to answer questions. Also, it is not appropriate to tip for questions which are answered by handing you a brochure to read.

Tip only for special free services such as spending considerable effort probing through timetables, guides and directories for you, phoning outside to make reservations for dining, calling outside for information or making special arrangements. In cases such as these a tip of one up to two dollars is appropriate.

Do not tip for services that are charged. For example, do not tip for purchasing tickets to ballgames, theatres or special functions. Generally, these are sold on a self-liquidating or profit-making basis and the clerk or house is probably making a sales commission. If you pay for whatever the hospitality clerk arranges, you probably should not tip for it.

Larger tips are appropriate when that money accomplishes a task you could not possibly do for yourself, such as obtaining tickets to a sold-out event. Sometimes a two to five dollar tip can accomplish wonders as an incentive for hospitality clerks to apply their special knowledge and contacts. Never, however, do you tip in advance.

Exercise Facilities & Diet Meals

A new service has emerged into the world of tipping. This is the service of exercise facilities and diet meals. Hotels, motels, resorts and convention centers are now providing exercise rooms, jogging trails, walking space and exercise machines and even room service for those people who are on an exercise schedule. This ties in with a new diet schedule and special meals. This has opened up a whole new field of tipping services. In some places the exercise equipment can be brought into the customer's room for privacy. Diet food is also provided for guests who require special service and the tipping can go back as far as the chef. Special equipment facilities are provided so people do not have to carry their own equipment. You can often rent or purchase what you need, including sweat suits, running shoes, and other gear.

All of this comes under the service person's jurisdiction and therefore, tipping is growing in this phase of service. For special attention, extra service and set up or take down of rental equipment, tip the usual 15%. For special services beyond the usual, you should tip a little more. Divide the tip between the service people if more than one service person is involved.

Computer Services

The hospitality industry that is composed of hotels, motels and resorts is making great strides in the improvement of service via the computer. Hotels are having computer terminals installed in thousands of rooms which provide services such as flight schedules, a directory of good restaurants in the local area, ordering flowers and other gifts, stock market information and, yes, even video games for pleasure. Some of these conveniences will no doubt eliminate some tipping and will decrease some of the duties of the bellboy and other hospitality people. The cost will probably be included in the cost of the room.

CHAPTER 7

***

Travel

Traveling will often present many new and sometimes confusing tipping situations. This chapter presents suggested tipping amounts and guidelines for handling service people you encounter while traveling by public transportation such as taxis, limousines, buses, and even wheelchairs; airlines; railroads; and cruise ships. Remember, these are suggested amounts, and you must carefully evaluate each situation to determine exactly what size of tip you feel is appropriate. We again repeat, as in Chapter 6, that the public and service industry must realize that in this country there are different wage scales throughout the country and various classes of people which will change the amount of tip.

TAXIS, LIMOUSINES, BUSES

Taxi Driver

Tip 20% on small fares; 15% on fares $5 and over.

Tip extra for special help such as maneuvering heavy and awkward cases and packages, carrying bags upstairs for you or into buildings, returning to pick you up at a specified time or for taking you to a remote location where the driver has little opportunity to pick up a return fare. Tip extra for asking a driver to wait for you.

Keep in mind the revenue the driver will miss during the time spent waiting. Also, you should tip extra for helpful information given above the level of casual conversation, and any services that require extra time and effort by the driver. Security is another benefit cab drivers can provide by waiting outside for the few moments it takes to see that you enter a building safely in questionable neighborhoods or late at night. If you wish the driver to do this be sure to ask specifically and tip the driver before alighting from the taxi. Taxi drivers, like other service people, depend quite heavily on their tips to complement their wages.

Airport Limousine Driver

No tip required if service is included in cost of your air fare.

Many limousines are owned and operated by airlines, and the drivers of these vehicles are generally well salaried and as a rule do not receive tips. This may be modified, however, if personal service requiring their extra time and effort is rendered to you. Then tip one to two dollars depending on the value you place on their service.

Independent limousine services, where you pay the driver a specific rate, are a different matter. In this case the driver operates on much the same basis as a taxi driver and does rely on tips. They differ from taxicabs, however, because limo drivers usually chauffeur more than one party at a time. Collectively, a small tip from each of several passengers can be quite handsome even though distances to and from an airport are often great. A one dollar tip is adequate if there are other passengers. If you are the only one, a two dollar tip is appropriate.

City Buses, Subways, Trains and
Commuter Buses and Trains

No tip is expected.

Drivers of these mass transit systems are salaried and do not rely on tips for a living. Neither do they provide special services such as help with luggage and bundles. They are paid to maintain tight schedules and remain at their driving posts.

If you are a regular passenger, however, you may wish to give your favorite driver a small gift at holiday time. You should hand it to the driver directly with a word of thanks and good wishes or use a sealed envelope for the gratuity with a note or card inside. There is no guideline for a gift such as this. Suggested amounts can vary from one to two dollars and up, according to the value you place on the service.

Interstate Scheduled Bus Driver

No tip is expected.

The drivers of regularly scheduled interstate buses are salaried, licensed and receive adequate payment for their service, without gratuities. They are responsible for loading your luggage into the special external compartments and carrying out all passenger regulations to provide safe travel.

Exceptions to the no tipping custom for these drivers may be if they agree to make an unscheduled stop for you or hold up departure of the bus to wait while you make a phone call at a scheduled stop. If you feel compelled to tip for such extra considerations, one dollar is not unreasonably high compensation for the cost in time, which will have to be made up somehow.

Charter Bus Driver

Tips vary by length of tour and number of passengers.

A one day or overnight bus ride with a full compliment of passengers may reasonably result in a collective tip of $20 or $30 from passengers to the driver. If two drivers are involved they will divide the tip if both travel with the group from departure to destination. If they switch drivers at a halfway point (the first driver leaves and a second driver comes aboard), tip each driver half the amount you plan for the complete trip.

For longer trips and tours, figure from 50 cents to one dollar per person per day depending on how helpful the driver may be. Often you will find charter bus drivers act as ex-officio tour guides giving interesting bits of information along the way. Some are chosen for their unique ability to informally join into the spirit of the tour in a quasi-host relationship. For drivers such as these the higher per day amount would be appropriate. When there is not a full busload of passengers for the charter run and if the driver-host has been exceptionally helpful and cooperative also consider the one dollar per day per passenger amount or a trifle more.

Bus Tour Guide

Tip 50¢ to $1.00 for short tours; $2 for day long tours.

For short tours of from two to four hours where you spend most of the time aboard the bus, tip 50 cents to $1.00 per person depending on the quality of the guide. You may want to tip more if considerable time is spent by the guide conducting walking tours at various points of interest. This requires much greater knowledge and extra care in keeping track of passengers while off the bus.

On full day tours, $1.00 is adequate per person when most of the time is spent aboard the bus. Consider $1.50 to $2.00 per person when much of the time is spent walking through points of interest.

Always evaluate the skill and knowledge of the tour guide before making your final tipping decision.

Redcaps, Skycaps and Porters

Tip 50¢ to $1.00 per suitcase,
up to 50¢ per small bag,
more for large and awkward luggage.

This tipping guideline includes taking your luggage from your point of arrival to your point of departure and helping you load and unload it. Just the act of getting it where you have to go is worth the amounts shown, provided it is done in a timely manner.

Consider tipping more when you have extra awkward parcels and bags. Tip extra for special favors such as asking the porter to go into the parking lot to help you load or unload, or when you ask the porter to wait while you pick up magazines or stop at the restroom along the route.

Porters are paid low wages, if any, and rely very heavily on your generosity for a living. Good porters, however, make good money because of the vital service they perform to relieve you from heavy burdens and free you to look after your travel arrangements.

If you have only one suitcase and wish the porter's help with it, consider tipping more if the distance you have to walk through the terminal is long. Remember, it takes as much of his time to carry one bag as it does to carry four.

Wheelchair Service

No tip to rental or check-out clerk.

Whether you rent a wheelchair or check one out at the free service desk, do not tip the clerk who arranges the chair for you. The only person you should tip for helping you and your wheelchair passenger is the porter you may hire to push for you. A one dollar tip is adequate for merely pushing the chair from point to point. Tip more if the porter helps your passenger into the wheelchair, and still more if the porter also helps your passenger out of the wheelchair. For assistance at both ends of the trip and for pushing the distance, consider a two dollar tip. Consider even more if waiting is involved and the porter's time is required.

AIRLINES

All major airlines maintain a no tipping policy regarding services by all salaried airline personnel. Your offer of a tip will be politely refused. For this reason follow these tipping rules for the following specific airline personnel you may encounter along the way.

Airline Steward or Stewardess

No tips.

Airline Ticket Agent

No tips.

Airline Baggage Agent

No tips.

Airline Gate Agent

No tips.

Often there are times when airline salaried personnel go out of their way to be of personal help to passengers. Stewardesses, for example, may be of great special help in cases such as when a passenger on board a plane becomes ill. They also give special help to mothers of small children who are having a difficult time tending to their youngsters. Often special comfort is given to passengers who have a natural fear of flying. In such cases, it is human nature to want to have some means of expressing your appreciation. The best method is, of course, a sincere thank you at that time, or before leaving the plane. Another means is to remember the airline employee's name and later write a special letter of appreciation to the airline general offices addressed to the Director of Customer Relations. In the letter, ask that your letter be forwarded directly to the person who helped you. If you do choose to write a letter of thanks be sure the service rendered was in keeping with normal airline policies regarding passenger services.

RAILROADS

Pullman Porter

Tip 50¢ to $1.00 per suitcase,
up to 50¢ per small bag or package,
more for large, bulky bags or trunks.

When you travel Pullman, check your baggage at the terminal and it will be delivered by the Pullman porter to your compartment aboard the train. Their work is complicated by crowded baggage car conditions and often they have to do their work quickly during short stopovers. It is well worth the amounts mentioned in the guideline.

Porters also do errands for you enroute. A customary tip is 50 cents (plus the purchase price) for bringing you a paper, 50 cents to one dollar for beverage set-ups and ice delivered to your compartment, in addition to the corkage price. Tip 50 cents to $1.00 for wake-up calls or special advance notice prior to arrival at your destination.

Generally, observe the same rules as you would in a hotel including a tip for preparing beds and tidying up compartments or berths.

Conductor

No tip unless special service is rendered.

Often the only railroad employee available to serve you in coach cars will be the conductor, who is normally busy with ticket duties and other official business. In many cases, however, they can help you with such comforts as pillows, reading materials and information. A tip of 50 cents is suitable. Should the conductor decline the tip, be sure to thank him and do not pursue the matter.

Elderly or disabled passengers often wish to tip the conductor for helping them to and from their seats or to and from restrooms and dining cars. There is nothing wrong with offering a 50 cent tip for such help, but if the tip is declined, a simple thank you is satisfactory. If you do plan to tip, remember that during long trips there may be a change of conductors which may complicate getting your tip to the right person. Keep this in mind in your decision as to when to tip.

Bar Steward

Tip 15% of the check.
For one drink, tip a minimum of 25¢ to 50¢.

This is a standard amount regardless of how you are served, either at your seat or at a central service bar where you pick up your own drinks.

Dining Car Waiter

Tip 15% of your check.

All six basic services are included in railroad dining cars, so the full 15% (2½% for each basic service) is appropriate. Give the tip when the waiter collects, either by leaving it on the tray or by giving it directly.

CRUISE SHIPS

Tipping is expected and encouraged aboard most cruise ships. There are some, however, that include tips in your total fare and still others that frown on tipping altogether. Before you sail, it is important to know the ship's policy. Remember, too, that the recommended tipping minimums on cruise ships encouraging tipping are just that — minimums.

Your travel agent or business agent for the cruise can supply all the information you need when you are planning your trip. If you board without asking about tipping policies, you can still relax, because the subject will likely be covered at a passengers' welcome aboard meeting, or in the printed information on ship policies that is distributed to passengers. If you forget to ask before boarding, miss the meeting and can't find the printed information, you can still ask the ship's purser or, if all else fails, ask your cabin steward directly.

Ships have different methods for tipping different serving people while on board. Some should be tipped as their services are rendered. Others should be tipped periodically or at the end of the cruise. The trick for you is to figure out the best way to use the practice of tipping to your own advantage and still comply reasonably well with tipping policies outlined by the ship.

The two most important people to remember are the cabin steward and the dining steward (or waiter). These people are in charge of your primary needs — your cabin and your meals. Just remember that because they are most important to you, they are also the ones you tip either periodically or at the end of the cruise. On short cruises, it is usually recommended that you tip them on the final day of the cruise. On longer cruises of more than ten days, it is often recommended that you tip periodically throughout the cruise.

One traveler said he thought the reason some ships request tipping be withheld until the final day was to prevent cabin and dining stewards from suddenly feeling too prosperous in the middle of a cruise and jumping ship at some exotic port of call. Regardless of how facetious the idea may seem, it does help illustrate that ships may really have good reasons for their policies that you had not considered.

Ships usually recommend minimum tipping amounts for the cabin steward and dining steward and it is a good idea to hang onto those minimums until the final day whether they ask you to tip periodically or at the end. It avoids misunderstandings in some cases. Some ships do query passengers on the last day if their cabin and dining stewards report they have not received their gratuities. Hopefully, the queries are to determine whether or not service has been satisfactory during your cruise. By withholding the recommended tipping amounts until the last day, you can assure yourself of the best service. Tipping early on the last day of the cruise, instead of at the last meal, brings lots of smiles which you can appreciate as a good tipper.

Serving people who are tipped as the service is rendered include the deck stewards, wine stewards, bar stewards or waiters in the cocktail lounge. Some ships have bellboys (or the equivalent) who serve in a variety of ways, and room service waiters who serve your champagne breakfasts or broth dinners on rough days at sea. These people work on a recommended percentage of the bill, or on a flat fee basis for simple errands.

There is one important variation for the latter people who bring service to your cabin. On some ships these people have different titles and work completely under the jurisdiction of the cabin steward. The titles are often cabin boy, junior cabin steward, assistant steward or night steward. It is important to know whether they work independently or under the cabin steward's supervision. If they do work independently, you tip them as their services are used. If they work under the cabin steward, they are not tipped. You tip the cabin steward, and he pays the others according to an established compensation plan.

If there is an exception to our rule about not tipping for future service, it would probably occur aboard ship. The situation is different at sea. A limited number of passengers are isolated in a limited amount of space (a ship) with a limited number of serving people, for what is often an extended period of time. These circumstances of being cast together seem to automatically bring about a more personal relationship with the serving people. In such a situation, tipping seems an ideal means of quickly establishing yourself as a reasonable, fair and generous person who is worthy of equal attention from the start. This is the reason we recommend tipping guidelines in excess of those published by most cruise ships.

The Cruise Lines International Association (CLIA) of New York and San Francisco, which represents some 27 member cruise lines, suggests you tip the cabin steward (or the equivalent) two dollars per person per day, and the busboy (or dining steward's assistant) one dollar per person per day. Wine stewards and other serving personnel should be tipped on the basis of 15% of their bills. This recap of CLIA recommendations is admittedly over simplified, but it will provide you with a reference point for comparison of the following guidelines which are designed to give you latitude in tipping in the interest of improved service while on board.

Cabin Steward

Tip minimum $2 per person per day.
Optional extra up to $2 per person per day.

The minimum is adequate for a cabin steward who works alone and whose work is limited to the care and maintenance of your living quarters. If his service is excellent, consider an optional extra of from 50 cents to one dollar per person per day. Save the recommended minimum of two dollars per person per day for payment on the final day and use your optional extra amount for a tip at the beginning and periodically throughout the cruise.

If your cabin steward has assistants who work under his supervision to provide basic housekeeping services as well as doing errands, bringing drinks, ice and foods, the recommended minimum is probably not really adequate. Consider tipping the cabin steward an optional extra amount up to two dollars per person per day, depending on the amount of service you require and the quality of the service. Do not tip the assistants, but tip the cabin steward periodically from the optional extra amount you plan to pay. Save the recommended minimum amount to pay on the last day of the cruise. The cabin steward will share the tips from you with the helpers to make sure they are also compensated for their work.

On occasion, you may feel compelled to tip one of the helpers directly for extra special services and considerations. Feel free to do this, but do it discreetly. Keep the transaction between the two of you. Such tips should not diminish the amount you plan to pay the cabin steward.

Dining Steward (Waiter)

Tip minimum $3 per person per day.
Optional extra, $2 per person per day.

The minimum is higher for the dining steward because an assistant works with the steward as part of a two person team. The three dollars per person per day recommended minimum compensates the dining steward at two dollars per person per day and the assistant at one dollar per person per day. Always tip the dining steward, who will pay the assistant according to their special arrangement. Consider saving the recommended minimum for payment at the end of the cruise. Tips given at the beginning or paid periodically should come from the recommended optional extra allowance, up to two dollars per person per day if service warrants.

Titles for this dining room serving team vary from ship to ship. Here are some combinations of titles you may encounter on your ship: waiter and busboy, dining steward and assistant steward, or senior dining steward and junior dining steward. One of these combinations will probably serve you almost every meal while you are on board, so you will come to know them well. You will discover the busboy, or assistant, does far more than merely clear away the dishes at the end of a meal. The assistant is part of the serving team and works under the close supervision of the dining steward. Extra tips to the steward also reward the assistants, but if you feel the assistants still deserve a little extra amount, feel free to tip them directly at the end of the cruise. An envelope bearing the assistant's name should be given directly or left with the purser of the ship.

Remember that the up to two dollars per person per day optional extra tipping recommendation adds up rapidly when there are two or more in your party. Do not hesitate to use fractions of this amount when calculating extra gratuities.

Wine Steward

Tip 15% of the wine bill.

When you pay for your passage on most cruise lines, the price includes all food, lodging and transportation, but it does not include such items as beer, wine and liquor. You are asked to pay for these when they are served and tip the people who serve them.

When the wine steward presents his bill at your table simply add 15% and give it directly or leave it on the tray. There are some fantastic wine stewards on ships and you will often feel compelled to tip extra for their service and a frequently exceptional selection. In many cases rounding your tip to the nearest higher dollar is sufficient. Otherwise, an extra 50 cents above the 15% amount is adequate.

Maitre d'hotel

No tips unless special service is given.

When special arrangements are necessary, the maitre d'hotel is the one who makes such decisions and can be helpful in many ways. If, for example, you wish to join a group not normally seated at your table, the maitre d'hotel may be able to provide an extra table for the purpose. The maitre d'hotel can make special arrangements for birthday or anniversary celebrations and help with other extraordinary needs. Base the gratuity on the time and effort put into fulfilling your request. Tip directly at the time of the request or remember to leave an envelope marked for the maitre d'hotel at the end of the cruise. Two to five dollars per occasion is adequate.

Section Captain (Dining Room)

No tips unless special service is given.

Certain dishes you order may require special attention by the captain of your section of the dining room. If tableside services are needed to bone the seafood, mix special dressings or flame desserts, it is appropriate to tip in much the same manner you tip the maitre d'hotel. You may tip directly when an opportunity arises, but do it discreetly; or you may remember the section captain at the end of the cruise with an envelope addressed with his name. One to two dollars per occasion is satisfactory. Base the tip on the time and effort it takes to perform the service.

Bar Steward

Tip 15% of the bill. Minimum 50¢.

More than this is welcomed but not expected. If you do tip more, it should be for services such as running a bar tab for you, paying by credit card (which takes extra time and record keeping), or for unusual services of some kind. The bar steward may relay messages for you, do special favors to make you comfortable or make some much appreciated introductions.

Keep in mind that foods served in the bar are usually included in your cruise cost and served at no charge even in the lounge. This often covers such beverages as milk or orange or tomato juice without alcoholic ingredients. If there is no charge for this kind of drink, leave a minimum tip of 50 cents, at least, for the service.

Deck Steward

Tip 15% of cost of any purchases you make.
Other services are on a flat amount basis.

There is usually no charge for towels at the pool, use of deck chairs or use of the shuffleboard courts, but the deck steward can be very helpful in arranging these for you. Base your flat amount tips on the time and effort devoted to your needs. Fifty cents to set up two deck chairs for you or to move them from the shady to the sunny side of the pool or the other side of the deck would be appropriate. Twenty-five cents should provide fresh towels for two people at the pool and 50 cents should get you next in line reservations on the shuffleboard court. Pay these tips as you go.

If you plan to spend a lot of time on deck, and know you will have special needs, you can often make advance arrangements with the deck steward to have your deck chairs placed in your special spot everyday. If you plan to make such arrangements, allow at least one dollar per day for your party of two. Pay part in advance and part at the end of the cruise, or periodically if service is excellent. Also, plan to pay extra for extra services rendered as you go.

If the deck steward also provides beverage service, tip him 15% of the bill with a minimum of 25 cents each time.

Public Room Steward (Game Rooms, Theatres)

Tip 25¢ to 50¢ per person on occasion.

The public room steward keeps the floors dry, the ash trays clean and generally sees to keeping theatres and game rooms clean. Occasional tips from 25 to 50 cents are appropriate and can be paid whenever you are using the rooms and see him.

Bellboys, Cabinboys, Room Service Waiters.

Tip 15% of the bill.
Tip flat amounts for "No Charge" errands.

Titles may vary on all ships — even ships from the same country — so it is difficult to know which titles prevail on the ship you are taking. Before you tip for any room services, make certain the server is not part of the cabin steward's staff. If the person works independently from the cabin steward, tipping is appropriate. Tip when served.

Tip 15% of the bill for drinks or something as mundane, but necessary, as a pair of socks from the ship's store. Most any trip they make to your cabin is worth 50 cents to $1.00. If 15% seems smaller than appropriate, increase the tip according to the time and effort given.

If you decide to hide out in your cabin and have breakfast or dinner there instead of the dining room, and if your food cost is covered in your passage price, tip $1.00-$1.50, plus 15% of the wine bill. If the food is not covered in the cost of your cruise, then tip the room service waiter a straight 15% of both the food and wine bill.

Deck Waiters

Tip 15% of the bill.

On some cruise ships the deck steward is the one who provides beverage and other such services, but on most ships these duties are handled by special waiters who make periodic rounds to see what you need. Tip them as their services are performed and base tips on 15% of the charges. No service on deck by these waiters is worth less than 50 cents, unless it may be for a package of chewing gum or similar item that can be picked up while taking care of another customer.

Bar-Lounge Waiter

Tip 15% of the bill.

If a waiter, instead of a bar steward, brings your drinks, tip the waiter. Follow the same rules as when tipping the bar steward, 15% of the beverage bill with a minimum of 50 cents, whichever is greater. Consider tipping extra for extra service such as keeping a bar tab for you or paying by credit card. Do not tip for foods or snacks served in the lounge for which you are not charged.

Croupier

No tips necessary.

Dealers at gaming tables do not expect tips. However, many people, whether motivated by gregarious nature or superstition, do leave a chip or two when leaving a table. If you feel compelled to do so, make certain the practice is acceptable aboard your ship.

Never tip a croupier before you play.

Tipping Estimates

It is difficult to make an estimate of your tipping needs based on the cost of your cruise. Prices can range according to length of cruise and also accommodations. Despite the rate difference, the food service and deck services available to passengers with any level of accommodations are identical on most ships. Only a few ships with a number of different dining rooms can make food services commensurate with the cabin class. Because of this, the only really successful way to estimate your tipping needs is to consider each possible tipping need you anticipate during the cruise, add them up and then, advisedly, add $20 or more to be sure. Time spent making a tipping estimate may prevent your having to rob other budget allocations to find money for tips.

One traveler who enjoys tipping for excellent service uses a system for estimating his tipping budget which we offer here for information purposes. First, find the figure exactly in the center between the most expensive and the least expensive passage offered by the cruise line. Then, determine 10 percent of that figure and this answer constitutes the tipping budget for the cruise. For example, on a given cruise, the middle point between $900 for a cabin and $4,500 for a suite on the promenade deck is $2,700 and 10 percent of that would give you an estimated budget of $270 to pay in tips during the cruise. This estimate would be high for many modest needs, but comfortable for most who enjoy tipping for excellent service.

Freighter Cruise Tipping

Traveling on a freighter cruise is not very different from other cruises, except for the number of passengers. Usually the number of guests is limited to the amount of space that is provided for passengers. There is also a closer relationship between passengers and crew. The meals are usually excellent, but not as plush as on a regular cruise ship. Most of the time the passengers are on their own and are not served in such a luxurious manner. The ports of call are usually different and the amount of sightseeing is usually left up to the passengers. Ground tours are not provided unless requested through the local tourist channels. Tipping, in general, is done at the end of the cruise. Evaluate the service received and tip according to the standard procedures as you would on any cruise. However, when the results of such closeness and companionship result in an especially meaningful experience, the tipping should be on the generous side.

CHAPTER 8

***

Miscellaneous Situations/ General Services

Included in this chapter are suggested tips for those many miscellaneous service situations that we all encounter. They are listed alphabetically for your easy reference.

Answering Service Operator

No tips, but occasional cash gifts from $5 to $10.

If you wish to reward a specific person on the staff, put the cash or check in a small envelope bearing the operator's name. Drop it off in person or mail it to the answering service in another envelope with instructions to deliver it to the proper person. If you have no specific person in mind, give or send the amount to the answering service with instructions for dividing it among the operator staff.

To make your gift more memorable, give it at holiday time or on other occasions you know will be meaningful to the operator, such as birthday, anniversary or just before vacation time.

Babysitter

Tip 15% when warranted.

Tips for babysitters are not customary. If they are good enough to warrant tips above the rate they have contracted for, the tip can be given at the particular time they proved to be more worthy. It would be better to hire them for the next time at a higher rate instead of having to rely on a tip.

For special times when they are deserving of a tip, 15% is a good standard to follow. Tip them for performing extra duties which do not conflict with their main duty, for enduring special hardships such as staying several hours later than agreed upon or performing exceptionally under unforeseen or difficult circumstances.

Barber — Stylist
Tip 15%.

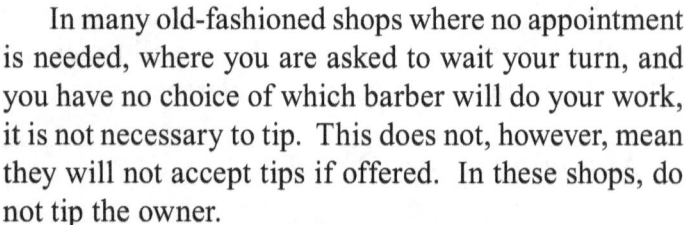

In many old-fashioned shops where no appointment is needed, where you are asked to wait your turn, and you have no choice of which barber will do your work, it is not necessary to tip. This does not, however, mean they will not accept tips if offered. In these shops, do not tip the owner.

Most barber-stylists who work by appointment and give very personalized service are accustomed to receiving tips. Fifteen percent is the standard amount whether your barber-stylist is the owner of the shop or not.

Beach Boys
Tip based on service received.

Beach boys should be tipped in accordance with the service provided, such as arranging and serving in cabanas and providing the essentials of the beach patrons. They act similarly to a waiter in a restaurant and should be tipped as such.

Beauty Salons
Tip up to 15% of the bill.

Titles in beauty salons can be confusing and are often created more for their promotional value than for use in identifying people who do specific work. In the interest of simplifying tipping for the customer in a business which has become a maze of different tipping rates, these basic rules are established as a minimum standard to follow when all services are satisfactory.

Regardless of title or work performed, tip a standard rate of 15% to stylists, shampooers, permanent specialists, manicurists and consultants. If they are paid individually for their work, tip them individually when you pay. If you receive a composite bill for their combined work, give one tip at the time you pay to be divided as shop policy provides.

Tip extra if you ask for such things as:

1. a special stylist or expert,
2. immediate appointments without notice,
3. service at a place outside their salon,
4. use of special products not stocked by the salon,
5. if you cancel and reschedule appointments frequently.

Tip extra if you ask them to photograph or make special records for your later use in the same shop.

Use 15% as the basis for all your tips. Extras should be given for good reasons such as extra time and effort on your behalf.

Caddy

Tip 15% to 50% of agreed fee.

The tip given depends on the going rate for caddy fees at the club where you are playing golf. If fees are high and a caddy turns in a satisfactory 18 holes, the 15% tip is adequate. If the club has no caddy fees, or very low ones, feel free to make your own agreement with the caddy and tip as much as 50% or more if the service has been exceptional. Caddies usually do the work because they love the game as much as you. Don't take advantage of them.

Car Wash Attendant

Tip 25¢ to 50¢.

The price of a car wash and the number of employees involved are not favorable to tipping. If you wish to tip, a flat fee of from 25-50 cents is satisfactory. Put it in their "tipping box" so they can all share the tip. If they have no "tipping box," give the tip to the person who delivers your car to you.

Catering Service

No tip if gratuity is included in bill.

It is customary for catered functions, weddings, pool parties, graduation and anniversary events that the catering service include all gratuities in the bill. This is often 15%. Always check before you give additional tips. If a tip is not included, a tip of 15% of the bill may be presented to the person in charge of the serving, with instructions to divide it between the serving people. Avoid individual tips unless it is apparent that singling out certain personnel is warranted. In that case do it discreetly. If you are also paying a gratuity in the bill, a small flat amount is sufficient for employees being singled out for extraordinary service.

If your event is catered by a charitable or civic group as a fund-raising project, a 15% gratuity over and above the agreed price is appropriate if service warrants. It is often wise to reserve judgement on a gratuity with such group arrangements until after the event, and it is agreed that service was satisfactory.

Clerks in Stores

No tips.

"No tipping" guidelines have been established for retail store clerks in the United States and many retail stores actually prefer that no tips be offered to their personnel. Gratuities offered to tailoring and alterations people or to retail employees involved in installing goods are sometimes successful, however, no guidelines are established. If the alteration or installation is routinely scheduled, do not tip.

Clowns

No tip for contracted services.

Clowns perform many tasks for various types of activities and functions, from birthday parties to Santa Claus to nightclubs. One of our Tippers International members is an active clown and a member of an association of clowns. He says that no tip is expected for family birthday parties and prearranged events. No tip is required whenever a clown's services are contracted for, because most places pay for these services as part of a sales promotion and the clown is being paid by the agency.

Tipping clowns in restaurants or nightclubs is appropriate. If the entertainer leaves an item at the table and spends at least five minutes at your location, it is suggested that a tip of one dollar be given. The amount will vary from this depending on the time and the enjoyment the customer has. The famous rule of "be generous, but discreet" would certainly apply here. Let the clown be the showman.

Custodians, Caretakers and
Building Superintendents

Occasional gifts appropriate.

Regular tipping for services is not recommended, but occasional gifts at holiday time or other meaningful times are appropriate. A gift of cash from five to ten dollars before holidays, birthdays or vacations is a thoughtful way of expressing your appreciation.

Delivery Services

*Tips optional. Not required if
delivery charge is collected.*

For a local or merchant-owned operation, a tip is optional, with an appropriate amount being 25 cents to one dollar if no service charge is added or collected.

Tip a local messenger or courier an optional one dollar to two dollars if no service charge is added for delivery.

For floral and gift delivery, one dollar to two dollars should be given if no delivery charge is added.

Regular delivery people, such as the butcher, grocer, dairyman, newspaper or laundry person, can be appropriately rewarded with small personal or cash gifts at holiday time or for special occasions such as prior to vacations, birthdays or anniversaries, depending on how well you know them. Five to ten dollars is adequate, but more is appropriate if exceptional service has been given.

Do not tip for freight or parcel service delivery. It is discouraged by many companies.

Repairmen and installers should not be tipped for routine work. Tip only for exceptional service such as emergency calls requiring personal sacrifices such as night work or weekend time.

Entertainers

Tip $1 to $5 for special requests.

Tipping for entertainment has survived through the centuries as one of the most gratifying forms of giving. There were the magicians who performed many magical feats for their kings and queens and the ladies in waiting. There were the tumblers and acrobats who performed in the same arena or courts. Most of these talented people worked and survived by their wits. They traveled alone or in groups. They were not on any payroll, but worked only for tips. In some cases where their acts or tricks were well accepted by those in power, they were able to find a home and settled in until they lost their favor and had to travel on.

These entertainers survived by receiving coins for their services. Groups got together and formed what we now call circuses. In the early days these talented families passed on their talents from one generation to another. Circuses were started in the European countries and, in order to survive, they began to charge fees for their services and entertainment. These fees were divided between the performers, some as partners and some just as wage earners. Entertainment was varied and specialized in forms of wire walking, aerial tricks, animal training and clowns. They entertained people of all ages and are still doing it to the present day, but in different arenas and forms.

The clowns and magicians were one field that received favors in the form of money. The other forms of entertainment included music, painting, poetry and writing. Most of these other services were drawn away from the pot of gold, so to speak, and became regular forms of employment. But the entertainers, clowns and magicians continued to survive on tips and gratuities.

Today, we still have these people who provide us with their services. In the entertainment field we have singers, musicians, piano players and bands. Some are in groups and some are individuals. Most of these people work for wages or residuals from the sale of their products. We also have singing groups on the sidewalks who still survive on tips. Remember the old organ grinder with the monkey?

As the monkey performed to the music he held out a cup and people would drop in coins. They survived on these donations which were forms of tips.

Now we have singing waiters, violin players, singing telegrams, vocal groups and bands. But, unless they perform something special, tips are hard to come by, because they contract for their wages from the establishment for which they perform. Special requests, however, require tips and these range from one dollar per request to five dollars for more, depending on the number of people involved.

Food Delivery

A tip of 10% of the bill is appropriate,
with a minimum of $1.00.

Consider increasing the amount of the tip if the driving conditions are difficult or the distance traveled is excessive.

Garage Mechanics And Service Managers

No tips are expected.

Tip only for special considerations such as helping you in an emergency situation or rescheduling other work to accommodate your needs on short notice. One to five dollars is adequate depending on the circumstances and the nature or size of the repair.

Gardener

Seasonal or periodic gifts instead of tips.

A gardener who spends much or all of the week working for you is more a regular employee than a service person. The gardener should be rewarded with more care than other service people who visit once or twice a week for a few moments. Weekly tips are not recommended, but seasonal or periodic cash or personal gifts valued at up to five percent of the total cost of the services are in order. For exceptional service you may wish to give more. This may be presented as either a gift or a bonus.

Grocery Carry-Out

Tip 50¢, if you tip.

Many grocers discourage tipping their carry-out people because they wish it to be a free service to their customers. If the store policy permits, and you feel generous, tip up to 50 cents. Consider factors of weather and the size of the load.

Hospital Aides and Nurses

No tips. Small gifts proper on occasion.

Refrain from giving cash gifts. Merchandise gifts such as candy, flowers or items of a meaningful nature are appropriate. Gifts may be given to individuals or to a group of the nursing and care staff. Holiday time or when leaving after a hospital stay are customary times for giving. Instead of a gift, consider giving a cash donation to a nurses' charity fund or hospital fund.

Housekeeping

Seasonal or periodic gifts instead of tips.

A good basis for reward to a good housecleaning person, whether full-time, half-time or part-time is five percent of the total amount earned. It can be given on special occasions such as birthdays, anniversaries, before vacations or at holiday time, or as a bonus at a certain time of the year. When exceptional service has been rendered with cooperative spirit and regularity, gifts of greater value may be appropriate. This person works very closely with the family and is hard to replace. Generosity often rewards the giver as well as the receiver.

Instructors

Non-formal education only.
Gifts appropriate at end of instruction.

Tips as such are inappropriate, but small cash or other small meaningful gifts are acceptable at the end of courses of many kinds, such as golf, tennis and other athletic instruction, trade skill courses, hobby workshops, self improvement and business courses. Gratuities given by individuals or collectively by a student group may range from $5 - $20 per individual up to $50 - $100 per group. These should be placed in an envelope addressed to the instructor, and given either in person, by mail or through sponsoring organizations. Personal gifts such as wearing apparel, briefcases or hobby equipment are also appropriate.

Very short courses complete in one or two days or with a very low number of total sessions seldom require a gift.

No gift of any kind is in order if you feel the instructor has in any way been inadequate or non-deserving. Do not be coerced by a student group. Give only if it is in keeping with your personal conviction.

Lifeguards

No tip.

Lifeguards are not usually tipped, except if asked to do special favors. Generally they are too busy watching the crowd to take on any special favors, but in some cases they will help out. Lifeguards are trained personnel who are responsible for the safety of the people at the beach or pool. They should not be distracted from their duties except for emergencies.

Limousine Rental Chauffeur

Tip 10% to 15% of rental fee.

If the chauffeur assigned by the rental agency to drive your limo has been congenial, efficient, helpful and obviously willing to cooperate to make your event successful, tip him in much the same way you would tip a taxi driver. Tip up to 15% for a short assignment, and up to 10% for a full day or longer assignment.

Movers

*No tip required, but occasionally
justified for unusual service.*

Moving companies frequently discourage tipping and a well planned move should provide little need to tip for extra demands you make. If your moving company approves, do it only upon successful completion at your destination. If you are especially demanding of the unloading crew, if you have them move heavy furniture two or three times before you find where it looks best, or if your arrival at the destination is several hours or a day later than promised and they have to wait for you, they are deserving of extra compensation. Base your tips on the amount of time and effort expended on your behalf to comply with your demands. If there are no delays and a modest amount of time is needed to handle special requests, $5 - $10 for two movers or $12 - $16 for four movers is adequate. Offer cash or the price of a good lunch.

Parking Attendant

Tip under certain conditions.

Do not tip booth attendants in lots where you pay for parking, but both park and retrieve your own car.

Tip up to $1.00 in lots and garages where you pay to have your car parked and retrieved for you.

Tip $1.50 to $2.00 in garages and lots where your car is parked and retrieved for you, but where you pay no parking fees.

Recreation Directors

Not usually tipped.

Recreation directors are usually not tipped. However, on special occasions they can be invited to take part in certain events that they control, especially at resorts and conventions where their services help make the convention a success. Those in public office are never tipped.

Rest Room Attendant

Tip 50¢ to $1.00 maximum for personal service only.

Do not tip the attendant for general cleanliness of the facilities. Tip only for services provided specifically for your individual benefit, such as cleaning a lavatory for your personal use, brushing your coat, providing individual soap for your use and handing you towels. Where disposable items are provided by the attendant, tip up to 50 cents for soap and towel, 25 cents for towel only or soap only. Tip 50 cents to $1.00 for providing individual cloth towels. Where services are deluxe, in shower rooms for example, which provide soaps, towels, lotions and personal grooming preparations, tip up to one dollar for pleasant, efficient service. Tip only on the basis of services you actually use.

Service Station Attendant

No tip unless special service or consideration is given.

Do not tip unless the attendant has been especially helpful in an emergency situation. It is also advisable to consider a gratuity to encourage an attendant to do special emergency or unscheduled work for you. Tip one to five dollars depending on the size of the job and the urgency.

Shoeshine Boy

$1.00 tip for shoes of one color.

Mens or ladies shoes of one color are less difficult to do, so a $1.00 tip is standard. Tip extra for two-tone shoes or ladies shoes which are strapped or styled with open toes or heels (when on foot). Shoeshining is swiftly becoming a vanishing profession. Do your part to sustain it.

CHAPTER 9
***

Conventions And Meetings

If you are planning a convention or a large meeting in any major destination, it might be a good idea to do some early planning. "Meeting News" reports that it is almost 50% harder now to get a booking than it was previously, although some resources believe it is about the same.

It is also being reported that some American companies are building meeting rooms and exhibits in semi-trucks and other types of vehicles and using them throughout the country. We personally were acquainted with a home building company that built a large trailer to do their promotions in the 1970's. We don't know of the success of the promotion from the trailer but we know that today they are one of the nation's largest home builders. This has proven to be a cost-effective way to hold meetings and business events. Tents can be furnished to provide for additional conference rooms. This, of course, changes the whole planning with the service industry.

"Help!" cries out one notable meeting resources coordinator of Rocky Mountain Association of Meeting Planners International. She is glad someone is coming out of the woodwork to set some standards for meeting planners everywhere. "How do we handle tipping for convention services?"

Many planners stew over how to distribute tips in such a way as to ensure the highest quality of service for the guests at the conventions and also to be fair to the employees who serve them. They don't want to short change anyone, yet they would like to avoid squandering their company's or client's money.

The big difficulty for the planner is the wide variety of situations with which they will be confronted. How many are attending the convention or meeting? How long is it being held? How many meeting sessions are being conducted? How much special assistance from the local staff will be required? In what region of the country is the convention or meeting being held? Is it at a resort or at a central city hotel or convention center? Is it in an area where union contracts dictate gratuities for some employees? How well are the various employees compensated by regular salaries? These and many more questions need to be addressed when considering how much to distribute in the form of tips. As each year passes, more and more questions and problems arise to frustrate meeting planners and companies who hold seminars and conventions. This applies to all planners whether they represent corporations, companies, private associations, public associations, or just the local scout troop.

The Convention Budget

It seems impossible to set up standard guidelines for tipping. So let's take a look at what must be considered when planning a convention or meeting, as shown on the Prime Consultants Convention Budget Outline. This outline starts with the convention budget. How much money do we have for this meeting? The listings by category are the basic costs, the blanket charges, the extra charges and federal, state and local taxes. But, we find that a new element, incentive gratuities, has arrived on the scene and could affect all the categories. It now seems necessary to supply an incentive program for the workers so you can be assured of good service for a successful convention. These incentives can be in the form of cash, gifts, trips, entertainment, or meals, and should be given to the best service person in each category. The incentives may be introduced by the company holding the meeting or the establishment providing the meeting facilities.

This incentive program can be worked in two ways. The convention center can determine and distribute the prizes or the meeting planner can handle the distribution through their own program. These incentives can be in lieu of tips or in addition to tips depending on how much is set aside for this purpose. This new concept for assuring a successful convention could be seen as a form of bribery to assure better service during the meetings.

Prime Consultants
Convention Budget Outline

Basic Charges

Guest Rooms – Single & Double – Food
Convention Hall Expense – Mailings – Postage
Guests & Speaker Expense – Hospitality Rooms
Transportation Expense – Telephone Expense – Gifts
Insurance Expense – Security Deposit – Souvenirs
Printing Expense – Building Cost – Awards

Blanket Charges

Union Contracts – Set-up Crew
Take Down Crew – Parking Attendant
Hostess – Head Waiter – Porter
Bell Hop – Bell Men – Desk Clerk
Bus Boys – Chambermaids
Cloak Room Attendant – Rest Room Attendant

Additional Blanket Charges

Union Contracts – Cartage People
Clean Up Crew – Door People
Banquet Manager – Food & Beverage Manager
Chef & Staff – Wine Steward
Bartenders – Captains
Maitre D' – Waiters

Specials

Special Gifts – Gift Catalog
Magazine Subscription
Letter of Appreciation
Personal Family Dinner
Lunches
Cash – Envelopes, By Check

Extra Charges

Waiter or Waitress (Buffet) – Catering Manager
Airport Luggage Handlers – Taxi Drivers
Limousine Service Manager – Bus Drivers – Drivers
– Valet
Convention Service Manager – Catering Manager –
Bartenders – Cash Bar
Sports Professionals – Entertainment – Pool Attendant
Cleaning Woman – Electrician – Carpenters

Extra Charges

Hospitality Room Attendants – Reservation Clerk
Front Desk Personnel – Information Desk
Telephone Operators – Secretaries – Typist
Cashier – Mail Clerk – Housemen
Candy & Confections – Florist – Security Guards
Special Messengers – Printer & Sign Maker

Extra Charges

Golf Course Attendant – Golf Caddies
Sight Seeing Trips – Style Show People – Ushers
Wheel Chair Facilities – Elevator Operators
Lost & Found Desk – Safety Deposit Clerks
Special Guests – Social Events – Speakers
Interpreters – First Aid

Extra Charges

State Taxes – Local Taxes – Entertainment Taxes
Restaurant & Meals – Drinks – Admission Tax
Lodging – Public Utilities
Photographers – Reporters – Radio
TV Personnel – Newspapers
Publicity – Magazines

Blanket Service Charges and Sales Taxes

Let's take a look now at who should be tipped and why. You should be aware that a large proportion of convention contract dollars include a fixed service charge to be distributed to those involved in food and beverage service. The amount tends to range from 15-20%. The California, Colorado, Texas, downtown Chicago and New York area tax may vary from 4% to 9% and tips may vary from 10% to 18%. This affects the budget considerably. It is doubtful if very many would consider a 20% tip because planners report very strongly that the economic impact is the most troubling area. This shows the variances around the country, which should be kept in mind.

In some cities, the percentage of gratuity is determined by the union contracts. As a result, you might well decide not to distribute additional gratuities to waiters, waitresses, busboys, bartenders, wine stewards, captains and others who might be beneficiaries of the fixed service charge.

In a way a blanket service gratuity is like a sales tax. Consumers know they have to pay it but can't be sure where it goes. One often wonders if the designated percentage of a food and beverage bill really trickles down to the waiters and waitresses and others who are supposed to get their share.

Special Gratuities

Therefore, if some employee has provided truly extraordinary service, you might consider giving that employee a special gratuity in addition to the blanket amount. For example, there may have been a provision made for cocktails, yet at the last minute the hotel or convention center is requested to set up a bar. In that case, it would be a good idea to reward those involved in the arrangements with a special gratuity.

You should always check to see who is covered by the blanket service charge. At some places even the director of convention services and the banquet manager are among the beneficiaries. As for those who do not benefit from the service charge, the planner will have to decide whether or not to leave them a tip if their service has benefited the meeting. For example, chefs and the people in the back of the house are not ordinarily among those who you need to tip. But you might want to recognize exceptional efforts or encourage a chef to extend himself beyond the ordinary. This can be done in different ways either by giving the chef the honor of sitting at the main table or perhaps a special toast to his culinary accomplishments. On special occasions, the chef and his spouse can be entertained at a special meal with convention participants.

Guests should be made aware that the blanket gratuities are added only to those meals that are part of the convention or meeting. If someone from the convention wanders into the coffee shop for a late night meal or snack, they're on their own. Tipping is their responsibility for all activities outside those scheduled.

Similarly, the service charge probably does not cover bartenders at a cash bar. But, if convention planners have set up a bar and have arranged that the cost be totally paid for, no tip should be given to the bartenders. In fact, in some convention centers bartenders have been instructed not to accept tips in such situations.

There are some places where you may be required to pay stipulated blanket gratuities beyond the food and beverage services. In some cities, for example, you may have to pay a fixed service charge to the bellboy. Sometimes that amount is dictated by their union. The amount tends to be greatest in the more highly unionized cities. Maids too, might be among those provided for by a predetermined service charge, especially at resorts.

Suggested Tips

There are also a number of other employees who provide services which may not be covered by such charges, yet you do not want to forget about them. Here are some suggestions to consider for these persons:

Bellboy — A typical amount given to a bellboy is $1.00 up to $2.00 for each person checking into the hotel or convention center and about $1.00 up to $2.00 for each person leaving. In expensive, high class centers the prices can go up perhaps $3.00 or more per person when checking in and checking out. Sometimes bellboys are not included in the blanket gratuity, so they should be paid separately. Usually at resorts the tip should be higher because guests come with more luggage and golf bags, and often stay longer than at city convention centers. At resorts, convention participants often arrive by bus and are separated from their luggage. In these situations it is a good idea for the convention planner to take care of the tips to the bellboys. The convention goers should be informed that the bellboys have been taken care of so that they do not tip them again. The bellboys too should be made to understand that they are receiving a blanket gratuity and it would be inappropriate for them to hustle tips.

Maids — Some planners report that though general tipping guidelines call for individuals to tip maids, most people do not. Perhaps this is because they are not as visible as some of the other personnel. Because of this oversight and the fact that maids are among the lowest paid employees at a hotel, a planner should consider assuming the responsibility of tipping for the convention goers. A commonly used guideline is $1.00 up to $2.00 per day per room when there are one or two guests in a room.

Cashier, Reservation Clerks, Front Desk Personnel — It is proper to tip some of these individuals if they have provided special services, such as taking care of unusual problems with room assignments, answering phone calls, running errands or taking messages.

Telephone Operators — There are so many individuals manning the phones that a regular tip is inappropriate. But you might want to make a thoughtful token gesture, such as sending flowers or candy with a note of appreciation.

Housemen — These individuals who set up your functions often operate behind the scenes at odd hours. As a result, it is easy to forget about them, but don't. They can make or break a convention. They might be there to put up your material and arrange seating and booth material, but when you want them to take it down, and they are not available — look out! Most of these people are paid minimum wages, so a good size tip of $15-$20 is really appreciated and well worth the investment. Some planners leave a blanket gratuity for the head houseman to distribute.

Secretaries — You may want to leave something for the secretaries if they provided special assistance. They may have done some typing for the convention, made restaurant reservations or handled other similar details. However, a company or association will often bring along its own staff to take care of such tasks. You may also want to tip the convention service manager's secretary for the help provided in convention preparations.

Convention Service Manager, Catering Manager, Head Houseman, Catering Captain, Bell Captain, Bartender — These people are also compensated by their regular salaries. These people are the key to a successful operation and it is a good idea for meeting planners to work with convention service managers and their staffs to find out who should receive tips.

Sports Professionals — At some resorts and special events at conventions or meetings, you might like to thank a sport celebrity, not always with cash, but with a company gift or a personal gift. This would apply for an invited celebrity (in addition to his fee), as well as a celebrity on the staff at the resort or meeting place.

Distributing Tips

It is a good idea for meeting planners to work with convention service managers to find out who should receive gratuities. Some convention managers will provide a list of employees who have taken part in the convention or meeting. Others who are employed should not be given gratuities if they are engaged in other activities and have nothing to do with the particular meeting. Sometimes there are two or more meetings at the same time and a careful study should be made to determine those who are involved and should receive tips. Some planners prefer to give a lump sum to the convention managers and give them the authority to distribute the tips. However, this puts an extra burden on the convention manager. You should not ask convention managers to suggest dollar amounts because they do not know what the budget figures are for gratuities. For example, for one convention $1,000 might be a large figure and for another, just a drop in the bucket. Some planners like to pay a small amount in advance to those employees who will help set up the convention hall and then promise more when they end the convention. But, this is paying for advance services. The best way is to pay tips and gratuities on the way out only.

It is very important to make your tips and your expression of thanks as personal as possible. You can do this best by putting the tips in individual envelopes with a handwritten note of thanks, written on a business card, business or hotel stationery. If possible, distribute the envelopes personally to each person. However, this will involve hitting all the various shifts. Also, the distribution may be hard to accomplish where there are a lot of employees. In cases like this, you can ask a hotel representative to distribute the envelopes. However, this person may not like being put in the position of being responsible for cash in envelopes.

It may be a good idea to get the signatures of those receiving the tips to make sure that the money does indeed end up in their pockets. You may also like to have this list for your records. Some companies require the signatures of recipients as proof that they received the money or gifts and that the planners didn't pocket it. This is also a good record of expenses for tax purposes. In some cases a list of service people is required and a company check is mailed to them for their rewards. This is one way that the right people will get their rewards, but it is not a personal reward and lacks the personal touch. Also, tips can be distributed to employees through the customer's master account. If it is done that way, it may end up as information in which the Internal Revenue Service might be interested. Needless to say, there are many individuals today who would rather get an envelope with cash inside.

Gifts may be given instead of cash, as a way of saying thank you. For instance, you might give a sample product or a special product such as a personalized gift. Some companies hand out show items left over from exhibits. But be careful. While you are just trying to express your appreciation, you may end up getting the employees in trouble. Gifts are often subject to security scrutiny and employees may need proof that they have been given the items and have not stolen them. Even a half finished bottle of champagne may cause problems for a maid who has received it as a gift. So check and see if you should also include written proof that the item has indeed been given to the recipient.

Another way to express your appreciation is by giving a gift certificate or asking the recipients to select a gift for themselves out of a book. There are books available that list selections of gifts within certain price ranges. This is especially helpful for someone who wants to give a gift but is not familiar with the area stores or is not sure what the recipient might like.

A simple letter of appreciation can also go a long way as a morale booster. So often, negative criticism is offered and positive comments are neglected.

Allocations for gratuities in the budget sometimes do not cover everything at the convention. Things can come up unexpectedly and some arrangements should be made to take care of these unforeseen circumstances. Appropriate handling of tipping takes a lot of time before and after the convention or meeting, but gratuities, if properly handled, can help make the difference between a mediocre meeting and an outstanding meeting.

Delivery Of Tips At Meetings

The survey indicated that the following methods were used by meeting planners to deliver the tips:
1. 72% delivered the tips in person.
2. 23% added the tips to the master account.
3. 4% delivered the tips to one person and asked the person to divide the tips among others.
4. 1% used other methods.

Many planners indicated they would not or could not give cash tips. They substituted a gift instead. The gifts included flowers, pen/pencil sets, digital alarm clocks, dinner for two, theatre tickets, calculators, letter of thanks or commendation, and many others.

Previous "Meeting News" Survey Reveals 12 Tips On Tipping.

1. Tip only for service above the normal call of duty. Don't tip out of habit. Expect good service and reward exceptional service.
2. You do not have to tip with cash. If your budget, organization or by-laws prohibit, consider a small gift or even a letter of commendation. Anything! But it is important to recognize, in some way, exceptional service.
3. Plan for your tipping in advance. Assume the staff will be exceptional and budget for it.
4. Determine the total amount of money you wish to distribute or the type of tip, if other than money, in advance. Put it into your meeting budget.
5. Sit down with the sales manager or department directors and get the names of all the people who will be working your meeting.
6. Find out from the sales manager, director of catering or other executive to whom, how much, how and when the automatic "gratuity" is distributed.
7. At the beginning of the meeting, introduce yourself to each person who will be working your meeting. (Do not tip in advance.)
8. Watch each person carefully during the meeting. If you must, take notes on who is doing extra — when, where and what. Substantiate your claim that the person deserves a tip. (Instruct your staff to do so, too.)
9. At the end of the meeting, sit down with your entire staff and review, one by one, the list of hotel personnel. Don't forget to add anyone who suddenly appeared and did an exceptional job for you. It is very important to carefully and thoughtfully evaluate each candidate on the basis of

the criteria shown under the heading "How to Determine the Size of Tip."

10. Give each person the tip before leaving for home. Reinforce that this is a special tip.
11. When you get back to the office, write letters of thanks to all involved if they did a good job. Don't overlook those that didn't get a tip, but did a good job anyway. Send copies to their bosses or the general manager of the hotel.
12. If you've forgotten someone, send the tip with the thank you note. It is never too late to tip.

How to Determine the Size of Tip

Most planners indicated that they had no tipping systems, but they generally awarded tips according to the following criteria:

1. Visibility of the person.
2. Duties above and beyond the normal job.
3. Attention to the group.
4. Courtesy, cooperation and response time.
5. Availability, punctuality, overall attitude and whether someone had to work overtime or not.

Meeting planners who do have systems followed four basic patterns:

1. Set dollar amount per attendee, usually $1.00 to $2.00.
2. Set dollar amount per sleeping room used, usually $2.00.
3. Additional percentage in the range of .025% to 1.5% added to the banquet/catering bill or the total hotel bill. This is a percentage beyond the gratuity.
4. Set percentage beyond the total meeting budget, in the range of a fraction of one percent to two percent.

To help the meeting planner determine the size of the tip, "Meeting News" previously suggested the following form.

Use This Form To Determine Size Of Tip

1. Was the person visible to you during most of the meeting? Did he/she ask you how things were going and volunteer help without being asked?
2. Did this person work extra long hours (before 8:00 a.m.; after 5:00 p.m.; or on weekends)?
3. Did this person perform duties which were outside his/her regular duties?
4. Did you have any special, last minute needs which this person carried out?
5. Was the person courteous and cooperative at all times?
6. Was the quality of service of this individual better than the quality you have received from people in the same position at other hotels?
7. Was this person excluded from the automatic gratuity? If not, how much did they receive?

Position	Name of Individual	No. of Yes Answers to Questions	Additional Comments	Actual Tip
Convention Service Manager	_____	_____	_____	_____
Assistant Convention Manager	_____	_____	_____	_____
Head Houseman	_____	_____	_____	_____
Assistants to Head Houseman	_____	_____	_____	_____
Catering Manager	_____	_____	_____	_____
Banquet Manager	_____	_____	_____	_____
Catering Captains	_____	_____	_____	_____

CHAPTER 10

***

International

Tipping, on the international level, is as varied and confusing as are the many languages. In some countries, tipping is against the law, in others it is optional (with some exceptions), while in still others it is not only expected, but required. In general, it appears that tipping is as well established almost everywhere in the world as it is in the United States. Abroad, as at home, tips are part or even all of some people's earnings.

The secret of correct tipping abroad is to tip to the local expectations of the service people. You should always tip in the local currency and remember that a smile and a thank you should always accompany a tip. Never feel embarrassed to ask about the tipping customs of a country. Americans tipping abroad are often criticized. Overtippers appear to be showing off, while undertippers appear to be arrogant and stingy. It is important to tip properly and, if anything, to be a little generous. Because tipping practices vary from country to country, and even from one region to another, it is a good idea to ask your travel agent about the current expectations of tippees in the countries you plan to visit.

In general, keep in mind that tipping abroad, as in the United States, averages about 15%. But, also remember that in some places of the world tips are added on to your bill in the form of a service charge, along with local taxes. This is generally true throughout Europe and in large parts of South America. Usually the bill will show if a service charge has been added. But look carefully, because sometimes the information is in very fine print and, of course, it will be written in a foreign language. Even if a service charge has been added, an extra tip of five percent and more is expected in many places to guarantee good service the next time around. And remember that in some cases, tipping can be an especially delicate business.

If traveling under the European plan, with meals not included in the room rate, you should tip as you go, with an average of 15%.

Under the American plan of travel, all your meals are included in the hotel bill. It is not necessary to tip each time you dine. The best plan is to estimate 15% of the total dining bill at the end of your stay or the end of each week for long visits, and divide that amount among those who have served you. The division should be proportionate to the amount of service provided. Usually the waiter or waitress receives at least half of the 15% and sometimes more, according to your own evaluations. When you leave you can give a tip to the head waiter according to the service given you. If the head waiter has done little, you can give a dollar or two, but if you have been provided special services and favors, five dollars a week is in order. For a short stay of one to two nights, it is not necessary to tip the head waiter. The rest of the service people, including the chambermaid should be treated in the ordinary way, with a dollar or two a week in a small hotel and up to five dollars a week in an expensive first class hotel. For room service, tip the room waiter 15%, in addition to the amount charged by the hotel for room service.

The same rules applied to the American plan above also apply to the modified American plan, where breakfast and dinner are included.

Senior citizens may want to be aware that in most cases, Medicare will not pay for medical care or supplies received outside the United States. There are some insurance policies that do provide emergency coverage during foreign travel. It might be a good idea to contact your insurance carrier before traveling abroad.

The world of travel is advancing so rapidly that since the time of this printing things could have changed. It is highly recommended that when traveling in strange lands, you should carefully plan your trip and be familiar with the money exchanges, the customs of travel and dining, and the recommended places to stay and visit.

Be sure to learn all the tipping requirements beyond those expected on tours or what is expected if you are traveling alone.

The following will give you some idea as to what to do in unfamiliar places and how to cope with situations that may be unfamiliar to the traveler.

Argentina
Monetary unit: 1 Argentina peso

Tips and gratuities have theoretically been outlawed in Argentina, but hotels and restaurants add a stiff 24% service charge and tax to all bills. But, to receive good service when returning to a restaurant, it would be a good idea to add a little extra for a tip beyond the service charge. A maximum of 10% of the cost is recommended, but sometimes five percent is enough if the bill is high. The same charges are added in a bar. One-fourth of the listed service charge is a fair rule of thumb for an extra tip at a bar. There is no need to tip cab drivers and they do not expect it. About a third of the drivers own their own cabs. If a tip is required, figure about 15% of the fare. Tips for barbers and beauticians will average about 10% of the bill.

Hotels, Restaurants and Night Clubs	**24% service charge and tax added**
Porters per Bag	**3 pesos**
Doormen, Concierge	**3 pesos**
Barbers and Beauticians	**10% to 15%**
Taxi Cabs	**15%**

Australia
Monetary unit: 1 Australian dollar

Tipping used to be a very touchy subject in Australia and the South Pacific, but things have changed and today tipping is expected, especially from foreign tourists. It is not necessary to be extravagant. Add 50 cents to the set charge for a porter at the railway station or shipping terminal. Small change should be left for the taxi driver or about 10% of the bill. Hotels and restaurants usually add a small service charge of about 10% to the bill. But, if not added, a 10% tip would be in order.

As a general rule, tipping for all other services would be about the same as in the United States. Chambermaids should be tipped two dollars per week and barbers and beauticians 10-15% of the bill. Some private clubs, social clubs and sporting clubs do not practice tipping. Some have a tipping pool to which you contribute, but if you are attending any functions it is wise to inquire of the policy. When in doubt, it is wise to tip to avoid any embarrassment. Generally, tipping is for special services only.

Hotels, Restaurants and Night Clubs	**10% to 15% service charge added**
Porters per Bag	**50 cents**
Doormen, Concierge	**50 cents**
Chambermaids	**2 dollars per week**
Barbers and Beauticians	**10% to 15%**
Taxi Cabs	**15%**

Austria
Monetary unit: Euro (formerly schilling)

Most hotels and restaurants include in their rates a 10-15% service charge and taxes. However, you will probably want to give a waiter an additional tip of 10% of the bill and the bartender 10% of the drink bill. Chambermaids should be tipped one euro per day. Porters and bellboys one euro, doormen one euro and taxi drivers 10-15% of the fare. Personal favors and extra services should be rewarded with a little extra.

Hotels, Restaurants and Night Clubs	**10% service charge included**
Porters per Bag	**1 euro**
Doormen, Concierge	**1 euro**
Chambermaids	**1 euro**

Barbers and Beauticians	**10%**
Taxi Cabs	**10% to 15%**

Bahamas
Monetary unit: **1 dollar**

In the Bahamas there is an inclusive gratuity system where a mandatory service charge of 15% is added to all bills. These service charges are collected and divided between the service people, but it does not assure better services to the customer. It is best to check if service charges are included to be sure of not being overcharged. Sometimes it is necessary to tip extra for special services such as handling large or heavy baggage. For this, the porter should be tipped 50 cents. Chambermaids are tipped up to 50 cents up to 1 dollar per day, barbers and beauticians 10% and taxi cab drivers 10%. You will find that the add-on gratuity is sometimes included in the price of the meal or service, and although the customer is aware of this it does not stick out on the bottom of the check like a penalty for having dined there.

Hotels, Restaurants and Night Clubs	**15% service charge added**
Porters per Bag	**50 cents**
Chambermaids	**50 cents to one dollar per day**
Barbers and Beauticians	**10%**
Taxi Cabs	**10%**

Belgium
Monetary unit: Euro (formerly Belgian franc)

A 15% service charge is usually included in your hotel bill, so that you do not need to give any of the staff more than a token tip. Also, most towns levy a small visitor's charge, as do nightclubs. If they do not, you should add a tip. Taxi fares are expensive, but the tip is included.

Hotels, Restaurants and Night Clubs	15% service charge usually included
Porters per Bag	1 euro
Taxi Cab	none

Bolivia
Monetary unit: Boliviano

There is a 25% service charge added to both hotel and restaurant bills. But it is customary to add another 5 to 10% as a tip. The porter will expect 40 bolivianos per bag.

Hotels, Restaurants and Night Clubs	25% service charge included
Porters per Bag	40 bolivianos

Brazil
Monetary unit: Real cruzeiro

At restaurants and nightclubs, a 10-15% service charge is usually added to your bill, but you should add another five percent. Hotels usually add a 10% service charge to the bill. Porters, doormen, elevator operators and chambermaids are accustomed to getting a small tip for their services. It is customary to tip at the time the service is performed or it can be done when you check out. When a taxi driver helps you with your luggage, a tip of 10% of the fare is expected. At barbershops and beauty parlors, a 10-20% tip is expected. Cinema and theatre ushers do not expect tips. Tip washroom attendants and shoeshine boys about what you would tip in the United States. At airports, the porters work on a tipping pool basis, so it is all right to tip the last porter who puts your bags in your car or cab. He puts the tip in a general kitty from which everyone shares.

Hotels, Restaurants and Night Clubs	10% to 15% service charge added

Porters per Bag	**3 real cruzeiros**
Doormen, Concierge	**2 real cruzeiros**
Chambermaids	**small tip**
Barbers and Beauticians	**10% to 20%**
Taxi Cabs	**10%**

Bulgaria
Monetary unit: Lev

Tipping is officially discouraged, but it is acceptable, with 10% a safe amount to leave. If special favors are required and are given, it is safe to tip those who perform these favors.

Hotels, Restaurants and Night Clubs none

Canada
Monetary unit: Canadian dollar

Tipping in Canada is the same as in the United States. As a general rule there is no add-on service charge and the average tip is from 10-15%. Porters receive an average of 50 cents per bag, one dollar for trunks and heavy luggage, chambermaids no tip for single nights, but one dollar a night for several days, and more for a week or longer depending on hotel quality. Barbers and beauticians are tipped 10-15% and taxi drivers receive an average of 15% of the fare. Check room attendants, washroom attendants, doormen, ushers and concierges are all tipped the same as in the United States.

In some regions of Canada, French is the primary language, so it would be a good idea to check with your travel agent to see if the area that you are traveling to is French or English speaking.

Hotels, Restaurants and Night Clubs	**15%, no add-on service charge**
Porters per Bag	**50 cents to one dollar**

Doormen, Concierge	**same as the United States**
Chambermaids	**same as the United States**
Barbers and Beauticians	**10% to 15%, extra for special service**
Taxi Cabs	**15%**

Chile
Monetary unit: Chilian peso

Restaurants and bars add 10% to the bill, but waiters and waitresses expect an additional 10% in cash. Taxi drivers do not expect tips, but for long trips or if you hire a cab for a long period of time to travel around the city, an additional tip would be in order, and should be given according to the service rendered. All taxis in the cities are metered.

Hotels, Restaurants and Night Clubs	**10% service charge added**
Taxi Cabs	**none**

China
Monetary unit: Yuan

There is no tipping in China proper. Tipping is considered rude.

Colombia
Monetary unit: Colombian peso

In many restaurants, bars and cafes, a 10% service charge is added to the bill. If it is not added, a 10% tip is suggested. At favorite restaurants where you request a special table or services, a 15% tip is advisable. Taxi drivers do not expect tips. Porters at airports and hotels are usually given 2,000 pesos for each piece of luggage. Chambermaids and hotel clerks are seldom tipped and locker room attendants at private clubs do not expect tips. At private golf clubs, the suggested tip for caddies is 30,000 pesos for 9 holes and 40,000 pesos for 18 holes. Shoeshine boys are everywhere and are very friendly. Tip the shoeshine boy about 10,000 pesos and give 2,000 pesos to anyone who will watch your car or clean the windshield. Some waifs sing or dance for people who are leaving restaurants or theatres. They look forward to a tip for their efforts.

Hotels, Restaurants and Night Clubs	**10% service charge added**
Taxi Cabs	**none**

Czechoslovakia
Monetary unit: Euro (formerely koruna)

Hotels and restaurants include a service charge of 10% in the better places and five percent in others. In popular restaurants, it is usual to tip by rounding up the bill. If you do not understand the bill, a tip of 10% would be more than generous.

Hotels, Restaurants and Night Clubs	**5% to 10% service charge included**

Denmark
Monetary unit: Danish krone

Hotels and restaurants include service charges and usually quote fully inclusive prices. You should tip only for special services or personal help. Washroom attendants get one krone. Taxi fares include the tip, so do not tip extra. Also, do not tip movie or theatre ushers or barbers.

Hotels, Restaurants and Night Clubs	**service charge included**
Porters per Bag	**4 kronas**
Barbers and Beauticians	**none**
Taxi Cabs	**tip included**

Ecuador
Monetary unit: Sucre

In hotels and restaurants, all prices are subject to a 15% service charge and tax.

Hotels, Restaurants and Night Clubs	**15% service charge and tax included**

Egypt
Monetary unit: Egyptian pound

Hotels and restaurants usually include a 10% service charge on all bills. Porters generally receive 5 pounds per bag and a little more if special handling is required. A normal tip for chambermaids is 10 pounds per day. Barbers and beauticians are tipped on percentages, which range from 10-15% of the bill. Cab drivers receive 10% of the fare.

Hotels, Restaurants and Night Clubs	**10% included**
Porters per Bag	**5 pounds**
Chambermaids	**10 pounds**
Barbers and Beauticians	**10% to 15%**
Taxi Cabs	**10%**

Finland
Monetary unit: Euro (formerly markka)

Hotels are not too high priced and the hotel service charge of 15% takes care of everything. Restaurants are also not too high priced if you stick to the regular menu. A 15% service charge in restaurants and nightclubs should be sufficient, so no additional tip is required. A general guideline in Finland is that you can tip for good service, but it is not expected. Tip porters, if available at train stations, one euro per bag. Bellboys and doormen are tipped one to two euro. Taxi drivers, ushers, washroom attendants, barbers and beauty salon attendants are not tipped.

Hotels, Restaurants and Night Clubs	15% service charge included
Porters per Bag	1 euro
Doormen, Concierge	1-2 euro
Chambermaid	none
Barbers and Beauticians	none
Taxi Cabs	none

France
Monetary unit: Euro (formerly franc)

France has many good hotels with prices fixed by law and posted. However, in some exclusive hotels, prices do not include the taxes or services charges, so it is possible that an extra 25-30% could be added to your bill. Tip bellboys almost everywhere in France. In luxury hotels in Paris, the bellboys expect at least one euro for each service. Tip the doorman two euros for getting you a cab. Leave 10 euros with the concierge depending on the hotel category and the length of your stay. Upon leaving, tip the chambermaid two to three euros.

The practice of adding a 12-15% service charge to the bill is common in restaurants and cafes all over France. When these service charges are added, it is not necessary to leave anything extra. But, most people leave a little extra, from one to five euros, depending on the size of the bill. If the wine steward, the sommelier, has been particularly helpful, you may wish to give him from one to two euros extra. Tip hatcheck girls and washroom attendants up to one euro. Tip theatre ushers a minimum of one euro per person, and increase this up to three euro per person if you are seated in very expensive seats. Tip cinema ushers up to one euro. Cab drivers should be tipped 15% of the fare. Barbers and beauticians should be tipped 15% of their charges. The minimum tip for rail or airport porters is around one euro per bag.

Hotels, Restaurants and Night Clubs	12% to 20% service charge added

Porters per Bag	**1 euro**
Doormen, Concierge	**2 to 3 euros for cab**
Chambermaids	**2 to 3 euros per day**
Barbers and Beauticians	**15%**
Taxi Cabs	**15%**

Germany
Monetary unit: Euro (formerly Deutsche mark)

In hotels and restaurants, service charges are included in all bills. Menus and wine lists automatically quote prices including taxes and service charges. The service charges on hotel bills are enough, but, if for any reason you wish to tip the employees, this is quite acceptable. For example, you may wish to tip the porter who brings in your bags. Also, you can tip the hotel concierge if you have been given special service. Although restaurant bills include 10% for service, it is customary to tip about 5% in addition to this amount. Also, taxi drivers should be tipped about 10%.

Hotels, Restaurants and Night Clubs	**service charge included**
Porters per Bag	**1 euro**
Doormen, Concierge	**1 euro**
Chambermaids	**1 euro**
Taxi Cabs	**10%**

Great Britain
Monetary unit: Pound

Some restaurants and most hotels add a service charge to the bill, usually 12 ½ -15%. If the hotels do not add a service charge, divide this amount among those giving service. Bellboys and doormen who call a cab for you are tipped separately 5 to 10 pence. Tip taxi drivers 10-15% or a minimum of 20 pence, cloakroom attendants about 10 pence, and railroad porters about 25 pence per bag. Railroad porters are not always available, so be prepared to help yourself to a baggage car and do it yourself.

Chambermaids, bellboys, bartenders, and others who give you special service or special consideration should be tipped 10% or a minimum of 10 pence.

Hotels, Restaurants and Night Clubs	**12 ½% to 15% service charge may be added**
Porters per Bag	**50 pence**
Doormen, Concierge	**tip separately 25 pence**
Chambermaids	**50 pence per day**
Barbers and Beauticians	**15%**
Taxi Cabs	**10% to 15%**

Greece
Monetary unit: Euro (formerly drachma)

Hotels add a 15% service charge, but a little extra is expected by service people. Restaurants and nightclubs add 15% to the bill and sometimes as high as 20% around the holidays and Easter time. In first class restaurants, you should tip an extra five percent. Leave the extra tip for the waiter on the plate, and some small change on the table for the busboy. Round off the charge on the taxi meter to the nearest euro.

Hotels, Restaurants and Night Clubs	**15% service charge included**
Porters per Bag	**1 euro**
Chambermaids	**5 euros per week**
Barbers and Beauticians	**10%**
Taxi Cabs	**included**

Hong Kong
Monetary unit: Hong Kong dollar

In Hong Kong a 10% service charge is added in hotels and restaurants. There is always an extra 10% expected beyond the service charge. All other service providers, such as barbers and beauticians, should be tipped 10% of the bill. Taxi drivers are tipped more for short trips and less for long trips. Be sure to check the meter and pay accordingly. There is plenty of transportation and most of it is reasonable. Rickshaws have a tendency to overcharge, so you must be careful with the tip. It is good to be knowledgeable about the types of transportation. Advice and information can be obtained from the first class hotels and the United States Foreign Office. They welcome your inquiries and offer great help.

Hotels, Restaurants and Night Clubs	**10% service charge included**
Porters per Bag	**$3 HK**
Doormen, Concierge	**$3 HK**
Barbers and Beauticians	**10% to 15%**
Taxi Cabs	**10%**

Hungary
Monetary unit: Forint

Tips are generally expected, in addition to any service charges. Hotel porters, waiters and barbers should not be given less than 10%. Taxi drivers should receive 15-20% of the fare.

Hotels, Restaurants and Night Clubs	**10%**
Porters per Bag	**100 forints**
Barbers and Beauticians	**10% to 15%**
Taxi Cabs	**15% to 20%**

Iceland
Monetary unit: Krona

Hotels and restaurants will add an all-inclusive service charge to the bill and extra tipping is therefore not expected and indeed may be resented. This is perhaps just as well, considering that the service charge and sales tax will add somewhere from 20-25% to the tab. Taxi drivers, hairdressers and washroom attendants are not tipped.

Hotels, Restaurants and Night Clubs	**service charge included**
Barbers and Beauticians	**none**
Taxi Cabs	**none**

India
Monetary unit: Indian rupee

India follows the British tradition in many ways. It does not have a rigid system of imposing a service charge on bills, but service charges are becoming more common in the larger cities. Some hotels and restaurants have not adjusted to the add-on system, so figure a usual service charge of 10%. Waiters and bellboys, like their counterparts elsewhere in the world, expect to be tipped for their services. A tip for a room boy is about 50 rupees per night in a good hotel where no service charge is added. Many hotels discourage tipping. Be alert and do not tip those service people who say that they may have been on duty and have done nothing for you. Tip only for extra service that is performed just for you in hotels and restaurants. Bellboys should be tipped 50 rupees per bag. Cab drivers are not tipped, unless special service is performed. Private drivers can be tipped 100 rupees on behalf of a party of three or four people. Do not tip the doorman unless he has worked for it by doing something special by request. Government run hostelries do not have a service charge. If you have an opportunity to use these facilities, it is proper to tip 100 rupees for each full day of your stay. Cloakroom attendants should receive about 50 rupees and a railroad porter 50 rupees per bag.

Hotels, Restaurants and Night Clubs	**10% to 12 ½% service charge may be added**
Porters per Bag	**50 rupees**
Doormen, Concierge	**none except for special favors**
Chambermaids	**100 rupees per day**
Taxi Cabs	**none expected 10% is OK**

Ireland
Monetary unit: Irish pound

The standard tip in Ireland is 12 ½%. Most hotels include this service charge on the bill, but guest houses do not. In more elegant establishments an extra tip is expected. It is common practice to tip porters, car parking attendants, taxi drivers, barbers, waiters and waitresses. To be on the safe side, tip as you would in the United States for these services.

Hotels, Restaurants and Night Clubs	**12 ½% service charge usually added**
Porters per Bag	**same as the United States**
Doormen, Concierge	**same as the United States**
Chambermaids	**same as the United States**
Barbers and Beauticians	**same as the United States**
Taxi Cabs	**same as the United States**

Israel
Monetary unit: Israeli new shekel

Hotels, restaurants and clubs add 15% to all bills, but tip an additional 10-15% for exceptional service. Porters are tipped 2 to 3 shekels per bag and chambermaids 4 shekels per day. Barbers and beauticians receive an average of 10% of their charges, more if special services are requested. Taxi drivers and theatre ushers usually do not accept tips.

Hotels, Restaurants and Night Clubs	**15% service charge added**
Porters per Bag	**2 to 3 shekels**
Chambermaids	**4 shekels**
Barbers and Beauticians	**10%**
Taxi Cabs	**none**

Italy
Monetary unit: Euro (formerly lira)

Service charges of up to 15% are included in all hotel bills and restaurant checks. A service charge is included in restaurant bills, but add another five percent for the waitresses and waiters in the cities and resorts. Taxi drivers expect about 10% of the fare.

Hotels, Restaurants and Night Clubs	**service charge included**
Porters per Bag	**1 euro**
Doormen, Concierge	**1 to 2 euro**
Chambermaids	**4 to 5 euro per day**
Barbers and Beauticians	**10% to 15%**
Taxi Cabs	**10%**

Japan
Monetary unit: Yen

There is a 15% service charge added to all hotel bills and restaurant checks. Porters receive 50 yen per bag. For barbers the normal tip would be about 10%.

Tipping in Japan presents some problems because it is generally frowned upon. Custom and a sense of delicacy cause individuals to be offended by having money handed to them directly. If a tip is to be given, it should be placed in an envelope or put in a position where others will not see it. Sometimes a tip is left on a tray or it is arranged to be given in a discreet manner. In Japan, tipping is not customary in most day-to-day procedures. Tipping causes Japanese people to feel like beggars. So, in most circumstances it is a good idea not to tip. Instead you might offer a small gift as a token of appreciation.

Hotels, Restaurants and Night Clubs	**15% service charge added**
Porters per Bag	**50 yen**
Doormen, Concierge	**none**
Chambermaids	**none**

Barbers and Beauticians	**10%**
Taxi Cabs	**none**

Kenya
Monetary unit: Kenyan shilling

Hotels and restaurants add a 10% service charge to all bills and checks. Porters receive 50 shillings per bag. Taxis receive from 50 to 100 shillings. Most other services are free of tipping.

Hotels, Restaurants and Night Clubs	**10% service charge added**
Porters per Bag	**50 shillings**
Taxi Cabs	**50 to 100 shillings**

Luxembourg
Monetary unit: Euro (formerly luxembourg franc)

Service and taxes are included in the bill, but for especially good service you might give an extra five percent. Taxi drivers expect a tip, whether they merit it or not. Hairdressers appreciate a tip.

Hotels, Restaurants and Night Clubs	**service charge and tax included**
Barbers and Beauticians	**appreciate a tip**
Taxi Cabs	**expect a tip**

Mexico
Monetary unit: Mexican peso

Tipping in Mexico is about the same as it is in the United States. Service charges are seldom added to hotel, restaurant and bar bills. Fifteen percent of the restaurant and bar bill is a good safe tip unless special services are required. Always keep some five and 10 peso coins handy because there are many opportunities to tip for services. But, don't over-tip. People are generally satisfied with the amounts shown below.

Bellboys are generally tipped 20 pesos for one bag or package, with 50 pesos for three or more bags or packages. Porters would be considered the same as bellboys, but for heavy luggage where special carts are required, it might be wise to add a few pesos. Leave 20-30 pesos per day for the services of the hotel maid.

Taxi drivers do not expect to be tipped. However, some people give the change left over from the bill. When attending major shows or sports events, ushers are usually tipped from five to 10 pesos. When parking in public places it is customary to hire car watchers. Tip them or the parking attendant five pesos. If your stay is long, it would be proper to tip five pesos per hour for car watchers or those in charge. Shoeshine boys are usually independent workers and their fee is usually 25-35 pesos which should include the tip, so no extra is expected.

There are many tour guides in Mexico. Some will meet individuals or groups upon arrival while others can be contracted for. The usual tip for this service is one American dollar per person. If the tour lasts three to four hours or a half a day, the tip should be increased to two American dollars per person. For any extended trips the tips can be increased up to four dollars per day and up to $20-$25 per person per week. The quality of the information the guide provides should also be a factor in determining the size of the tip. Usually the guides do not take care of the bus driver, so it is proper to take up a collection for him at the end of the tour.

Hotels, Restaurants and Night Clubs	**15% no add-on service charge**
Porters per Bag	**20 pesos**
Chambermaids	**20 to 30 pesos per day**
Barbers and Beauticians	**10%**
Taxi Cabs	**none**

Morocco
Monetary unit: Dirham

Porters try to get as much as they can, but the official rate is three dirham per large piece of luggage and two dirham per small bag. It is sometimes cheaper to have a taxi take your luggage even a few blocks than it is to hire a porter.

In Tangiers, tip as usual, but taxi service leaves something to be desired. Sometimes the meter works and sometimes it does not. If there are five or six passengers in one trip from the airport to the hotel, the cost will be about 40 dirham. No coach service is provided. Dicker on the price of travel and distance and give no tip unless the driver is helpful and honest.

Hotels, Restaurants and Night Clubs	**15% no add-on service charge**
Porters per Bag	**3 to 4 dirham**
Doormen, Concierge	**10 dirham**
Chambermaids	**4 to 5 dirham per day**
Barbers and Beauticians	**5%**
Taxi Cabs	**none**

Netherlands
Monetary unit: Guilder or Florin

Hotel prices now include a 15% service charge. Tip porters and bellboys one guilder per bag or per service, especially if it is personal. The doorman will expect a similar sum for calling a cab. Taxi fares generally include a 15% service charge, when indicated on the meter. But, it is usual to give the driver any small change or even out the total. Most restaurant checks and nightclub charges include a 15% service charge. Hatcheck girls expect 25 cents to one guilder, depending on what type of place and number in your party. Washroom attendants receive from 25-50 cents. Tips for hairdressers and barbers are included in the price. Rail or airport porters should be given one florin per bag.

Hotels, Restaurants and Night Clubs	**15% service charge included**
Porters per Bag	**1 guilder**
Doormen, Concierge	**same as porters**
Barbers and Beauticians	**tip is included**
Taxi Cabs	**tip is included**

New Zealand
Monetary unit: New Zealand dollar

It is neither customary nor necessary to tip. However, a small tip for personal service in a hotel or restaurant would be a welcome courtesy. Cab drivers are never tipped.

Taxi Cabs	none

Norway
Monetary unit: Norwegian krone

Norway is not accustomed to much tipping, particularly outside the main centers. Service charges are always added to the bill in hotels, restaurants and bars. Round out the bill if you wish and, of course, tip for special service. Porters are usually tipped three kroner per bag. Beauty parlors do not expect tips. Taxi drivers do not expect tips, but if in doubt, give a small amount.

Hotels, Restaurants and Night Clubs	service charge added
Porters per Bag	3 kroner
Barbers and Beauticians	none
Taxi Cabs	none or small tip

Paraguay
Monetary unit: Guarani

It is customary to give a 10-15% tip on top of the charges that are placed on hotel, bar and restaurant checks.

Hotels, Restaurants and Night Clubs service charge included

Peru
Monetary unit: Nuevo sol

Service charges of 10% are added to most restaurant bills, but an additional tip of five percent is expected. Taxi drivers do not accept tips.

Hotels, Restaurants and Night Clubs	**10% service charge added**
Taxi Cabs	**none**

Philippines
Monetary unit: Philippino peso

Hotels, restaurants and nightclubs usually have a 10% service charge added to the bill. But, sometimes it is necessary to add extra for special services. Doormen can be tipped 50 pesos. In larger towns like Manila, porters receive tips ranging from 25 pesos per piece of luggage. In barbershops and beauty parlors, a 10% tip is the norm. It is not necessary to tip taxi drivers.

Hotels, Restaurants and Night Clubs	**10% service charge added**
Porters per Bag	**25 to 50 pesos**
Doormen, Concierge	**50 pesos**
Barbers and Beauticians	**10%**
Taxi Cabs	**none**

Poland
Monetary unit: Zloty

A service charge is usually added to restaurant bills. If not, add 10%. Tipping is not obligatory, but readily accepted. Cab drivers get 10% of the fare. Porters should be tipped an amount similar to other European countries.

Hotels, Restaurants and Night Clubs	service charge usually added
Taxi Cabs	10%

Portugal
Monetary unit: Euro (formerly Portuguese escudo)

Hotels and restaurants charge a 15% service charge and a three percent tourist tax, both are usually included in the price list. Waiters will expect extra tips. Taxi drivers expect 15-20% of the fare. Barbers and beauticians are usually tipped 15%.

Hotels, Restaurants and Night Clubs	15% service charge and 3.1% tax included
Porters per Bag	1 euro
Chambermaids	1 euro per day
Barbers and Beauticians	15%
Taxi Cabs	16% to 20%

Puerto Rico
Monetary unit: Dollar

It is customary to tip 10-15% in hotels, restaurants and nightclubs. Porters receive 50 cents per bag, doormen receive 50 cents to one dollar for services. Do not tip ushers. Barbers and beauty operators receive an average of 10-15%, as do cab drivers.

Hotels, Restaurants and Night Clubs	10% to 15%
Porters per Bag	50 cents
Doormen, Concierge	50 cents to 1 dollar
Barbers and Beauticians	10% to 15%
Taxi Cabs	15%

Romania
Monetary unit: Leu

A 12% service charge is added to meals in most restaurants, but leave something extra, about 10%, if the service is exceptionally good. Taxi drivers should be tipped from five to 10%.

Hotels, Restaurants and Night Clubs	**12% service charge added**
Porters per Bag	**small tip**
Taxi Cabs	**5% to 10%**

Russia
Monetary unit: Rouble

Suggested tips for waiters are five percent and for porters about 30 roubles.

Hotels, Restaurants and Night Clubs	**5% to 10% service charge may be added**
Porters per Bag	**30 roubles**
Taxi Cabs	**20-30 roubles**

Singapore
Monetary unit: Dollar

Restaurants, hotels and nightclubs usually have a 10% service charge added to all bills. Porters receive 1 dollar per bag, more if bags are heavy and special handling is involved. Doormen and ushers receive 1 dollar as a normal tip. Barbers and beauticians receive 10% on an average. It is not necessary to tip taxi drivers.

Hotels, Restaurants and Night Clubs	**10% service charge and tax added**
Porters per Bag	**1 dollar**
Doormen, Concierge	**1 dollar**
Barbers and Beauticians	**10%**
Taxi Cabs	**none**

South Pacific
Monetary unit: Various

Tipping is not customary and is not encouraged. In places such as airports, hotels and restaurants, signs are posted in several languages. In Tahiti, tipping is contrary to Tahitian hospitality. However, in large hotels the employees will accept tips and so will the tour guides and drivers.

Spain
Monetary unit: Euro (formerly peseta)

Service charges of 15% and taxes are included in the price of hotel rooms, but you should leave the chambermaid up to 10 euros a week and tip the porter about one euro per bag. If you call a bellboy, give him up to one euro. Spanish restaurants usually add a service charge to your tab, but you should also leave at least five percent extra, even when it says "service and tax included." Waiters in nightclubs will expect more. Taxi drivers get 10% of the fare.

Hotels, Restaurants and Night Clubs hotels	incl. 15% service charge
Waiter	5 to 10%
Porters per Bag	1 euro
Doormen, Concierge	1 euro
Chambermaids	up to 10 euros per week
Barbers and Beauticians	15%
Taxi Cabs	10%

Sweden
Monetary unit: Swedish krona

Hotel prices include a 15% service charge. Bigger hotels also charge extra for porter service, in which case porters do not have to be tipped. Inquire whether the porter service will be charged or not when you arrive at the hotel. A porter should be paid three kronar per bag. The service charge in restaurants is 13 ½% automatically added to the bill. Late at night the service charge is higher. Hatcheck girls and washroom attendants get two or three kronar. Cab drivers are always tipped at least 10% of the fare on the meter. Ten to 15% is paid in barbershops and beauty salons.

Hotels, Restaurants and Night Clubs	15% included in hotel bills
Porters per Bag	3 kronar
Doormen, Concierge	3 kronar
Barbers and Beauticians	15%
Taxi Cabs	10%

Switzerland
Monetary unit: Swiss franc

By law, an automatic service charge of 15% is now included in all hotel, restaurant, café, bar and hairdresser bills. This normally covers everything. However, some people like to give additional tips. For example, give the hotel baggage porter one franc, or three francs for a lot of luggage. Also, if anyone is especially helpful you can give an extra tip. If the hotel porter saves you money or gives you good advice on tours or recommends good restaurants or night spots, an extra reward is well spent. And if you feel that you have had special service from your hotel maid, you can leave her about five francs. Station and airport porters get 1½ francs for each article, plus 10%. In a cloakroom where no fixed charge is made, you should give about 50 centimes per person to the attendant. Fifteen percent is already added to taxi fares in most places. Ushers and washroom attendants expect one franc.

Hotels, Restaurants and Night Clubs	15% service charge included
Porters per Bag	1 franc
Doormen, Concierge	1 franc
Chambermaids	1 franc per day
Barbers and Beauticians	10% to 15% included
Taxi Cabs	15% included

Taiwan
Monetary unit: Della

There is a 10% add-on charge for service. Porters are tipped per bag provided they help you with your luggage. Beauticians and barbers are about the only other service people who receive tips. Their tips average about 10%. Tipping in Taiwan is not a regular custom, but service people are now expecting extra cash for services performed. Tip only for direct service.

Hotels, Restaurants and Night Clubs	**10% service charge added**
Porters per Bag	**small tip**
Barbers and Beauticians	**10%**
Taxi Cabs	**none**

Thailand
Monetary unit: Baht or Tical

Hotels, restaurants and nightclubs all have a service charge of at least 10% plus tax added to their bills. If you need extra service, it is customary to add an extra five to eight percent. In places where they add the tax, but not a service charge, 10-15% is a normal tip. Porters should be tipped twenty baht per bag.

Hotels, Restaurants and Night Clubs	**10% service charge plus tax added**
Porters per Bag	**20 baht**
Barbers and Beauticians	**10% to 15%**

Tunisia
Monetary unit: Dinar

Tipping is expected, even though the hotel bill says that everything is included. Tip the room maid or room boy a small token depending on the class of your hotel. Tip the same for the waiter and 500 milliemes per suitcase for the porter. If you are looking for guides in the country, be sure to make a deal with them before accepting their services. Watch for tricks to get tips.

Hotels, Restaurants and Night Clubs	**service charge included**
Porters per Bag	**500 milliemes**
Chambermaids	**token tip**

Turkey
Monetary unit: Turkish lira or pound

A service charge of 15% is added to the bill, but it does not always find its way to the personnel. Keep this in mind and tip those who have looked after you and give the tip to them personally. Waitresses expect about 10%. Washroom attendants, movie and theatre ushers will be thankful for a tip in the equivalent of about 25 cents. There is no need to tip taxi drivers as they overcharge in a most outrageous manner.

Hotels, Restaurants and Night Clubs	**15% service charge added**
Porters per Bag	**1 lira**
Doormen, Concierge	**1 lira**
Chambermaids	**5 lira per day**
Taxi Cabs	**none**

Uruguay
Monetary unit: Peso

Hotels and restaurants bill guests extra charges starting from about 10%. These are supposed to be tips, but are actually what they consider wages for their service people and employees. These people then expect another 10% on top of the bill. The extra charges are usually distributed among all workers, except elevator operators, on a point system. Tipping should be based on United States currency, with 80 cents to one dollar for handling two pieces of luggage at airports or other places of arrival and departure. Tip 10% for taxis and 30 cents for theatre ushers.

Hotels, Restaurants and Night Clubs	**10% added**
Porters per Bag	**80 cents to 1 dollar for 2 bags**
Taxi Cabs	**10%**

Venezuela
Monetary unit: Bolivar

Tips are usually left to the consumer's judgement, but in the majority of places for dining and drinking, 10% is already added to the bill. Tip bellboys and chambermaids about 1,000 bolivares for their services. In Caracas hotels, tip as you would in the United States, but tip less elsewhere. Taxi drivers are not tipped unless they carry suitcases. Gasoline station attendants usually are tipped for their services.

Hotels, Restaurants and Night Clubs	**10% usually added**
Porters per Bag	**1,000 bolivares total**
Doormen, Concierge	**1,000 bolivares**
Chambermaids	**1,000 bolivares**
Barbers and Beauticians	**10%**
Taxi Cabs	**none**

Yugoslavia
Monetary unit: New dinar

Most hotels and restaurants add on a service charge, but additional tipping is generally accepted at a rate of about 10% in hotels, restaurants and for taxi drivers.

Hotels, Restaurants and Night Clubs	service charge included
Taxi Cabs	10%

Conversion Charts

When traveling abroad, it's not always easy to know the difference between Fahrenheit and Celsius, inches and centimeters, or a size 8 and a size 38. We've put together a few easy conversion charts to help you measure distance, calculate weight, or just stay within the speed limit.

Length & Distance Conversion Chart
Length / Distance

In = Cm	Cm = In	Mi = Km	Km = Mi
1 = 2.54	1 = 0.40	1 = 1.61	1 = 0.62
5 = 12.70	5 = 2.00	5 = 8.05	5 = 3.11
10 = 25.40	10 = 3.90	10 = 16.09	10 = 6.21
12 = 30.48	12 = 4.70	50 = 80.47	50 = 31.07
		100 = 160.90	100 = 62.14

Weight & Volume Conversion Chart
Weight / Volume

Lb = Kg	Kg = Lb	Gal = L	L = Gal
1 = 0.45	1 = 2.21	1 = 3.79	1 = 0.26
5 = 2.27	5 = 11.02	5 = 18.93	5 = 1.32
10 = 4.54	10 = 22.05	10 = 37.94	10 = 2.64
50 = 22.68	50 = 110.23	50 = 189.70	50 = 13.20
100 = 45.36	100 = 220.46	100 = 379.40	100 = 26.40

Temperature Conversion Chart

°F	°C
32	0
40	5
50	10
60	15
70	20
75	25
85	30
105	40

Clothing Chart & Sizing Differences

Men's Suits & Overcoats

American	British	Continental
36	36	46
38	38	48
40	40	50
42	42	52
44	44	54

Men's Shirts

American	British	Continental
14-½	14-½	37
15	15	38
15-½	15-½	39
16	16	40
16-½	16-½	41

Women's Suits & Dresses

American	British	Continental
8	10	38
10	12	40
12	13	42
14	16	44
16	18	46

Children's Clothing

American	British Ht(in)/ Age	Continental Ht(cm)/ Age
4	43 / 4-5	125 / 7
6	48 / 6-7	135 / 9
8	55 / 9-10	150 / 12
10	58 / 11	155 / 13
12	60 / 12	160 / 14

Men's Shoes			Women's Shoes		
American	British	Continental	American	British	Continental
8	7	41	6-½	5	38
8-½	7-½	42	7	5-½	39
9-½	8-½	43	7-½	6	39
10-½	9-½	44	8	6-½	40
11-½	10-½	45	8-½	7	41
12	11	46			

PART III

The Public Responds

CHAPTER 11

***

Public Attitudes
About Tipping

We are in support of the free enterprise system of tipping. In this book we have provided the tools for people to use to bring tipping back to its original concept. We do not believe that gratuities should be added onto any bill for services you have not yet received, unless the services are contracted for in advance. We do not feel that the public should be obligated to subsidize anyone's wages, through tips, when the service is mediocre or poor. Tipping should be voluntary, with the tipper exercising the freedom of the final word. This is certainly the attitude of the general public also, as documented in the following comments and survey.

Don't Take A Tip for Granted

A noted columnist received a letter from a reader who wrote that they were in a restaurant and the waiter brought their check on a tray in the customary fashion. A few minutes later, the cashier came to their table saying he had to close out his cash drawer and requested that they pay their bill, even though they had not finished their lunch. They looked at the check and saw that it totaled $18.02. They placed two 10 dollar bills and two pennies on the tray for easy change. The cashier picked up the tray and never returned with their change. They were considering a tip of 20%, and were wondering if the cashier assumed the extra two dollars was the tip. The advice given by the columnist was that the waiter or cashier should always return the change no matter how much or how little it is. In a situation of this sort, it would have been within their rights to ask for their change. A tip is not an obligation and the amount should always be left to the discretion of the diner.

Tipping makes lots of people uncomfortable. They don't know how much to tip, or when, or when not to. However, most of us today feel obligated to tip even if the service is somewhat less than prompt. We tip out of habit, perhaps to avoid embarrassment. Tipping, at least for now, seems inevitable. Many who travel extensively find that tipping is the most annoying problem they encounter.

What Do Service People Want From Us

 Interviews with service people have been conducted to determine how much they are getting for tips. A random sampling from some interviews indicated that one waiter averaged tips of about 15% or better. A waitress reported that she received tips of 10% for breakfast, 15% for lunch and at times as high as 20% for dinner, with an average of 15%. A bartender reported average tips of 10% of the tab, while a club manager reported that a lot of people don't think to tip when they are drinking. A hairdresser reported a dollar as a normal tip. However, higher tips are recorded in the more elite beauty salons. A cab driver reported a dollar tip for a short distance, but a percentage of 10-15% when the trips get longer. A lot of non-tippers were reported. A skycap stated that there are no standards for tipping, but that they usually get about 50 cents to $1.00 per bag or a little better if there is excess baggage.

In general, the service people were pleased with the tips they received. They have accepted smaller tips with good grace, realizing it is an occupational hazard.

Tipping is very important to the serving people — tippees. Their tips could be 50% or more of their income. A service person can afford to work for minimum wage or less if they are lucky enough to be employed in a place where they take home $30-$80 a day in tips.

It is almost impossible to get service people to discuss their tips openly because tips are taxable income. They don't want to go on record and have the Internal Revenue Service find out how much they really make.

Tipping is not wholeheartedly endorsed by the food service industry. The feeling is that it is ridiculous to leave a tip for service personnel who sometimes spend less than a minute taking and delivering a food order. Only a sincere and caring service person deserves a tip. Restaurant management is not entirely blameless in the matter of tipping. Throughout the industry, service employees are recruited and hired with promises of substantial amounts of income from tips, which prompts service employees to expect substantial tips, whether they deserve them or not.

Tipping Is Not Accepted By Everyone

Articles have appeared in newspapers the past few years in which people expressed themselves openly on tipping. One person's feeling was that tipping was "illogical, unfair and uneconomic." People wonder "Why tips?" The postman, the salesclerk, the supermarket cashier do not get tipped. Others ask why the tip is based on the cost of the meal instead of the cost in time or the quality of the service. Why should a guest in a restaurant become an employer and face a dilemma over the size of the tip? They feel it is unfair. Others feel that tipping is demeaning to the tippee as well as the tipper.

There is a surprisingly deep resentment over tipping, but there are also a lot of people who are resigned to it and who continue to be confused about how much, to whom and when. If service is not good, it is not only correct, but it is very important, to register disfavor by reducing the tip. It is, after all, payment for services rendered. Unfortunately, it takes more courage than most of us gather to hold back a tip.

An article in a leading newspaper advocated the following technique to express dissatisfaction with service. For eight cents you could purchase a "zero cent" coin which said "give nothing — get nothing" on one side and on the other side said "this coin is your tip — it matches exactly the value of your service." Yes, there still is a lot of controversy in tipping. However, we do not advocate this method of showing your displeasure with service given. It is better to leave nothing than to leave something so blatant that it is an insult to the service person.

One of our members who has traveled extensively through 50 countries on business, reports that most of his distasteful experiences in entertaining his clients have been in the United States. His feeling is that in most cases in the United States, the waiters don't deserve the minimum wage, let alone the extra tip.

He objects very strongly to the 15% tip, particularly on limousine service. He feels that when gas prices go up, so do the limousine fares, and theoretically, so do the tips. So, he claims tips are being piggy backed and for that reason he does not tip 15%. He further claims that tipping is a "cash business" and that much of it is probably not reported on tax returns, so the tip is actually worth more than what you give.

Lastly, he thinks waiters are similar to his friend in the real estate business. His office gets seven percent of the sales price. So, as inflation causes houses to increase in value, it also causes his commission to go up. Similarly for the waiter's and limousine driver's tips. All three get more for no more service rendered.

One of our close friends at Tippers International feels quite strongly about tipping and expressed himself as follows:

"I cannot, in good conscience, approve the practice of tipping! Tipping degrades the human dignity of both tipper and tippee.

Immediately after the first contact between waitress and customer, a relationship is established which is similar to master and serf. The waitress must put on a happy face and maintain a jolly and friendly composure even though there is a temptation to spill the soup on an abusive, ill-tempered loud mouth who she is required to please. She is now serving two masters, the customer and her employer. If she responds in a manner that will restore her dignity, there will be no tip; but worse, her employment will be terminated. And why not? After all, she can be replaced by another for less than two dollars an hour.

Thus far I have dramatized a situation that tends to degrade the tippee or waitress. Moreover, this type of situation is encountered very frequently. The tipper or customer is not immune from assaults upon their dignity. Imagine, if you will, a middle class business professional treating several business friends and/or associates to dinner. We will assume that this person is not rolling in "dough" and is fastidious in justifying every expenditure.

After examining the menu, the host is shocked that there has been another increase in price, let alone the tip from which there is no apparent escape. A sense of resentment is beginning to build. The business professional also wonders how the increase of the standard tip from 10% to 15% can be justified. Being adept with figures and knowing that the cost of eating in a restaurant has risen at a faster rate than the overall cost of living, the professional determines that the real money earnings from tips are more than they were prior to the surge of inflation. The answer seems incomprehensible and adds to the frustration.

Shall that host base the tipping judgement on economic reality and compensate the waitress accordingly? What about assuming the position of a critic and sitting in judgement of the waitress's performance? Why not consult the guests regarding the tip? No, the probability of being labeled a cheapskate is too risky! Better play safe and pay the full 15%. By now this business host's personality is altered, the soup is cold, and he would be willing to exchange the salad for a Rolaid."

A report from another quarter indicates how professional some of our serving people are. They offer advice on dishes and wines. They take great pride in seeing that people enjoy their evening out and do their best to please. They truly deserve a tip.

Tippers International Survey

A survey of 2500 general consumers was conducted by Tippers International which was felt represented a cross section of people from many social and economic backgrounds. The results of the survey were very interesting.

The questions asked and the responses received are presented here.

1. Do you feel obligated to leave a tip for services?
Yes 71%
No 29%

Tipping has become a part of our culture and a tradition. However, it should be based on the type of service. We should not feel obligated to tip. There is no obligation to give a tip and the person who gives one enjoys the freedom of the final word. Tipping is a free will decision that benefits everyone in ways probably more important than money. The tippee has the immediate satisfaction of knowing the service was appreciated and the tipper enjoys the very human glow of his generosity plus the freedom to be the judge.

2. What percentage of the cost for the service do you normally tip?
00% 2%
10%...........................22%
15%...........................64%
20%............................1%
More 1%

A recent national survey somewhat disagrees with our survey of 2,500 consumers.
0-5% 10%
up to 10% tip............18%
up to 15% tip............35%
up to 20% tip 26%
more than 20%...........6%
unknown....................5%

It has been questioned by many people why the increase of 10% to 15% when the cost of food and services have gone up quite rapidly. Based on this fact, they feel that the tipping should have stayed at 10%.

In the survey 11% believed that the tip should be 20%. We agree that if there is extraordinary service given, it is proper to increase the tip, but it is not an obligation. We know that this happens in more expensive hotels and in areas where more affluent people live and visit.

3. What is your primary criteria for tipping?
Service......................50%
Courtesy 24%
Friendliness 15%
Food..........................7%
Other..........................4%

The response was somewhat of a surprise, as we felt the "service" percentage would be higher. The two traits of "courtesy" and "friendliness" could be considered part of the service, but this indicates how important courtesy and friendliness are to the general public. Apparently food is not used very much as the criteria for judging service, and we fell this is only fair, because the service people usually have no control of the food and they should not be penalized or rewarded based on the quality of the food. Of course, it is important how the service person handles any complaints. If you receive food you consider to be below par, it should be returned and courteously replaced with an acceptable substitute.

4. Do you feel service people expect to be tipped?
Yes 95%
No 5%

The answers here were expected. We know that for many services, tips are considered part of the service person's wages and we suspect that the general public knows this as well. In the service industries it is known that some of the people are making less than minimum wage, with this amount being paid by the proprietor.

The balance to bring the pay up to the minimum wage is made up by tips. There are, of course, exceptions to this type of set up.

There is a definite sign that more and more people are expecting to be tipped along with the traditional waiters, waitresses, doormen, bellboys and cabbies. There are other hands which are stretching out toward your pocket, like the janitor, engineers in high rise buildings, people who deliver dry cleaning, window cleaners and security guards, among others. The list is virtually endless. It was expected that 86% of the work force will be in the service sector. This is up 18% from 1980 statistics. What part of this sector will be looking for rewards?

5. Do you feel tipping should be left to the discretion of the consumer?

Yes 94%
No 6%

We, of course, fully agree with these responses. Considering this strong feeling, we wonder, how the idea of adding a 15% service charge to bills (particularly in restaurants) ever originated. Our feeling still is that tipping is not an obligation, but a right to be exercised by the consumer.

Tipping is a phenomenal system which originated to fill a need which exists yet today. It is a powerful motivational force to people in the serving profession, providing incentive, initiative and reward. It works without need for regulation of any kind because it appeals to the generous nature of consumers and preserves the customer's right to be the final judge of whether services rendered were satisfactory.

6. Do you feel an automatic service charge should replace tipping?

Yes 9%
No 91%

This is another question that received a very strong answer. The question relates to questions five and seven, and all deal with free will tipping as opposed to the automatic service charge. We wonder if any of the establishments that have started automatic service charges have even made any surveys to determine the feasibility of this change. Do they merely assume the public just accepts this change? Some of the restaurants are now applying a gratuity of 18% if 6 people or more are served. We wonder the justification of this amount – what was this based on?

A tip is not an obligation and must always be left up to the discretion of the consumer. Only then can a tip be a reward for service rendered. Tipping is a merit pay system voluntarily accepted by both parties. The preservation of this concept is the primary objective of Tippers International. A management decision to add service charges to restaurant bills does not constitute a tip in the pure sense of the word. Such arbitrary additions are nothing but surcharges levied to subsidize labor costs. These involuntary tips lessen the serving person's need to be sensitive to the customer's individual likes and dislikes and in no way guarantees better service. And, it can often dull management's perception of customer reaction. When the customer is denied the right to judge service quality, the whole concept of tipping is destroyed, along with the incentives it offers.

7. With an automatic service charge, would service be
Better........................5%
Same.......................23%
Worse.....................72%

We agree with this response, because the automatic service charge would take away the incentive to perform better. This might not apply, of course, to the larger and finer restaurants in the country, but it would certainly apply to the majority of the establishments that serve the greatest number of people.

How Much Can We All Afford to Tip

We have revised our book to make it as inclusive as possible. It is so easy to say the tips should be so much but we have people in different stations in life and some can pay more and some will pay less, depending on their income.

There are 10 basic occupational groups in the United States totaling 144,014,000 people employed as follows in round numbers:

Professional and related occupations	27,700,000
Service occupations	26,600,000
Office and administrative support occupations	23,900,000
Management, business, and financial occupations	15,500,000
Sales and related occupations	15,200,000
Production occupations	11,200,000
Transportation and material moving occupations	9,600,000
Construction and extraction occupations	7,200,000
Installation, maintenance, and repair occupations	5,600,000
Farming, fishing, and forestry occupations	1,000,000

The second largest occupation as you can see are the service occupations and they pay the least which is as little as $7.28 per hour. Do we expect them to afford a tip as large as the professionals who rank first in employment and at about $87.00 per hour? This of course, excludes the professionals such as attorneys whose rates go up to $300.00 per hour. The same may very well apply to the fourth largest occupational group – management, business and financial occupations who average a wage of $20.00 to a high $66.00 per hour while the production occupations vary from an average of $8.54 to $24.00. That is the reason we had to set up some range.

Prime Consultants made a recent survey to find out how much the people in the various occupational groups tip. Listed here are the findings:

1. Physical Therapist Tip

     If in a nice restaurant with six basic services provided in a very professional and excellent manner 20%

     If service is not up to par 15% or as low as 10%

2. <u>Housewife – Single with Children</u>
   If service is good in one of the nicer restaurants
   Was a waitress at one time.
   Respects the occupation. 20%

   If service not that good 10%

   If in regular restaurant and kids are along – <u>must</u>
   be offered beverage without asking. 15%
   If not, tip will drop.

3. <u>Office Person with Certain Financial Difficulties</u>
   In an affluent restaurant with six basic
   services provided in a very professional
   and excellent manner. 15%

   Family restaurant – full service 10%

   Buffet maybe nothing to $1.00

4. <u>Blue Collar Worker</u>
   If service is good in nicer restaurant or in a family
   restaurant and service is good to excellent.
   Makes no distinction between the type of restaurants
   but expects excellent service. 15%

   Keeping to 15% because he feels that prices have gone
   up so there is an increase in tip. Does not believe it
   should go up to 20%.

5. <u>Senior Citizens and Retired People</u>
   If an affluent or family restaurant –
   makes no distinction 10%

   If women go out in group and doesn't matter what the
   bill us, the tip per person is $1.00

If husband and wife go out and have an extra good time, the tip may be 10%

6. Bankers

If in affluent or family restaurant and service is excellent, the tip could be as high as 20%

If service is not that good, tip may be reduced to 15%

If service is bad, the tip may be nothing and Management would be notified of dissatisfaction 0%

7. Shop Management

In an affluent or family restaurant, no matter what the bill would be the tip per couple would be $5.00

Minimum would be 10%

8. Executive

If in regular family restaurant and the six basic services are provided in a very professional manner, the tip would be 15%

If in affluent restaurant and the service is excellent 20%

If service is just ordinary 15%

9. Our next personal interviewee, who is a traveling executive, gave us a very comprehensive report on how he tips. We would rank him in one of the higher occupational groups. His report and tipping habits are as follows:

Ed,

Below are my thoughts on some of your tipping questions. As I went through the questions, I noticed that in several cases I don't tip, i.e. door persons. Maybe I'm just cheap...or just don't run into these situations. I can say that I do tip whenever I receive excellent service like in the case where a service station attendant changes a headlamp for me on a rainy night or at Starbucks when the server is cheerful and polite.

As in all cases where you are traveling abroad or in a few cases domestically, be sure to check with local custom procedures appropriate for the location of your travels. In some areas, for instance Sweden, tipping is an insult and all charges are included in your bill. However, I generally tip as follows:

Waiters, Waitresses,and restaurant tipping:
>Full service finer establishments: 15% - 20%
>Full service cafes and lunchrooms: 15% - 20%
>Buffets or Cafeterias: Usually I leave $2.00 for the clearing staff otherwise I don't tip in these cases.

Some establishments automatically add a tip to your bill if there are more than 6 or 8 people. Be sure to check your bill to see if a tip or "service charge" has already been added. Also, if you are using a coupon or gift certificate, be sure to tip as if you had paid for your meal.

>Valet parking: $1.00 to $2.00 each time your auto is parked and retrieved. This amount should be adjusted higher if parking is particularly difficult or scarce.

>Cloakroom attendant: $1.00 per garment.

>Bathroom attendant: $1.00 per visit.

>Host or Hostess: I don't usually tip these separately from the wait-staff.

>Bartender: A $1.00 per round is appropriate otherwise tip as per wait-staff above.

Hotels, Motels, and Resorts:

Baggage handler or courtesy bus driver also handling your bags: $1.00 - $2.00 per bag.

Valet parking: $1.00 to $2.00 each time your auto is parked and retrieved. This amount should be adjusted higher if parking is particularly difficult or scarce.

Bellhop: $1.00 - $2.00 per bag.

Room service (if no service charge has been added): 15%-20%. Be sure to check your bill to see if a tip or "service charge" has already been added.

Maids: I always like to leave between $2.00 and $5.00 per day depending on the hotel.

Travel:

Baggage handler or courtesy bus driver also handling your bags: $1.00 - $2.00 per bag.

If the courtesy bus driver is not handling your bags: $1.00 - $2.00 per trip.

Taxi: It depends; generally I round-up on the bill which equates to a tip of no more than $5.00 per trip. However, the amount really depends on the difficulty of the travel and how friendly the driver is.

All others: use your discretion, ask questions and tip appropriately for the circumstances. For example, if you are golfing in an exclusive club with influential colleagues and important clients, tip the bag handler generously for the best overall impression. In many cases tip money is well spent particularly if you plan on returning often!

You will note how important excellent service is, yet this is not always provided. We are sorry to admit that in most of our experiences it has been mostly average. The services industry could learn a lot by reading our chapter on "Providing Good Service."

Just recently we had some experiences which are not very complimentary.

1. Coffee was ordered with a meal thru a waitress who was getting an education in Nursing. Later she asked if I wanted a refill and I said yes, in a little while. She stated that she would come back. She never came back but was seen chatting in the kitchen. I don't think she was much of a waitress and I don't think I would ever want her as a nurse.

2. We ordered a meal which included biscuits. This was repeated when order was being placed. Meal was served without biscuits and there was no sight of waitress. We had to hail down the manager to get our biscuits.

3. My wife ordered water with a lemon from a waitress. She was served later by another waitress without lemon. No use of causing any commotion.

4. Another common blunder, if you might call it as such, is when waitress or waiter serve coffee. Instead of serving it from the right side of guest, they just set it down close to the center of the table from any direction. This doesn't happen in the affluent restaurants but mostly in family restaurants. These procedures are overlooked but that does not make them correct or proper.

5. Serving the wrong order to a person when there are only 2 people being served. This mistake is understandable but is not proper.

6. Proper silverware not at table. Had to be asked for.

CHAPTER 12

***

Tipping Questions
And Answers

Most people at some time in their lives have found themselves in a tipping situation and were not quite sure what to do. The results could be embarrassing to both the tipper and the service person and also unfair to the person who depends on tips for a living.

Over the years, Tippers International has received thousands of inquiries regarding the art of tipping. These questions have come from individuals who were confused by a new experience in tipping. They have also come from service providers who wished to communicate to the world what they expect from their customers. We receive questions from large corporations seeking to establish tipping policies for their employees. Many organizations have also sought information to share with their members concerning advisable practices for tipping.

The wide range of concerns that have been expressed to Tippers International indicates the extent of confusion and frustration that tipping situations can cause. Consequently, this chapter will consist primarily of questions we have received regarding specific tipping situations and the recommendations of Tippers International.

Dear Tippers International:

I am writing to inquire about how much I should tip hairdressers. I feel that their bills are already terribly overpriced and I sometimes have no extra dollars. At most franchises, the standard layer cut is $20.00. Body perms are $45.00 to $85.00 depending on hair length. I now have *a regular hair stylist and wonder what is expected. Also, what's the least I could tip and still keep my self respect? Finally, must I tip at all?*

And another person writes from Phoenix:

Gentlemen:

I have a tipping dilemma which makes me dread going to the hairdressers. I have the owner cut my hair. He charges $30.00 for the cut. My hair is shampooed and rolled by his assistant. The total charge is $75.00. Since I can only afford to do this once a year, the tip is crucial! I've read that shop owners aren't tipped, but should I tip the person who shampoos and sets my hair 15-20% of the total cost? Or, what tip would you recommend in this case, and who gets what?

I read about your organization in the Sunday paper and it said "for more information write to" giving this address, but I will certainly understand if you can't answer individual questions of this specific nature. Still I would appreciate any help you might give me.

Both of these are honest questions that come from opposite corners of the United States. Both writers need some help and guidelines to follow so they will feel that they are doing the right thing. Our answer was:

Dear Madam:

Concerning tipping in beauty salons, keep two things in mind — tipping is a merit pay system to reward good service, and it is totally your prerogative to tip or not to tip. The normal tip is 15%, but can range from 10-25% when special services and favors are performed.

Sometimes titles in beauty salons are confusing, often created more for their promotional value than for use in identifying people who do specific work. In the interest of simplifying tipping for the customer, in a business which

*has become a maze of different tipping rates,
these basic rules are established as a minimum
standard to follow when all services are
satisfactory.*

*Regardless of title or work performed, tip
a standard rate of 15% to stylists, shampooers,
permanent specialists, manicurists and
consultants.*

*If they are paid individually for their work, tip them
individually when you pay. If you receive a composite bill
for their combined work, give one tip at the time you pay to
be divided as shop policy provides.*

*Tip extra if you ask for such things as: 1. a special
stylist or expert, 2. immediate appointments without notice,
3. service at a place outside your salon, 4. use of special
products not stocked by the salon, 5. if you cancel and
reschedule appointments frequently, 6. tip extra if you ask
them to photograph or make special record for your later
use in the same shop.*

*Use 15% as the basis for all your tips. Extras should be
given for good reasons such as extra time and effort given
on your behalf.*

*Regular customers often choose the more modest rates,
but are consistent about it when service is satisfactory.
Frequently, people who tip regularly on the low end of the
scale will add a small gift on holidays and birthdays for
encouragement, which raises the relationship to the valued
customer level.*

These situations exist in every town, village and city. They
also occur in nursing homes, hospitals and on cruise ships. Each
has a different level of pricing and service. Where prices are
higher, such as in resort areas, the tips increase. When prices rise
to beyond your range, there is nothing wrong with patronizing a
less expensive place.

Here is an inquiry from the service point of view:

Dear Sirs:
  I am a bellman at a resort in Kentucky. I understand you are part of some organization for tipped employees. I wish you would send me some information on this. Also please send ABC Corporation information on this. Their employees are terrible tippers.

The Kentucky bellman needed help on what to expect from hotel guests and singled out ABC Corporation visitors as most adept at not rewarding his services. Our response was:

Dear Bellman:
  The general rule is to tip the bellman 50 cents to $1.00 per suitcase or bag, up to 50 cents for small cases, extra for very large bags or trunks.

A bellman is an important person and should be treated well. The above guidelines can be and should be modified when circumstances are based on time and effort. If the bellman does more than escort you and your luggage from the lobby to your room, consider upping the tip. For example, if you are met at your car, your luggage is loaded onto a cart, the bellman waits while you check in at the desk, and then escorts you to the room where your luggage is placed on racks, and your garment bags are hung up, reward the bellman for this extra time and effort.

A bellman is an excellent source of information, too, and since you spend a few moments together enroute to your room, the opportunity is there to tap the bellman's knowledge about things you will need, and places you want to go. Good information is another consideration when you decide to tip.

Apply the guideline amounts and then consider the extra time, effort and information given you. A good tip upon arrival wins you a willing worker during your stay. However, never tip for future service. Also, remember that if you have only one bag and the bellman carries it to the farthest room in a large hotel, the 50 cents per bag guideline may not be enough.

It is surprising how these people pick guests that are knowledgeable in the art of tipping. As in this case, it is not good public relations to have representatives of a large corporation ignore any service person regardless of their position. You should always be discreet in handling situations and should be knowledgeable in the art of tipping and a little on the generous side. These people have an important job to do and should be compensated according to how they fill your needs and according to the standards of the people you represent.

A representative of a large corporation wrote to us with the following request:

Dear Sirs:

We are a meeting management department. We need some guidelines on gratuities. The groups we handle range from 15-2500 people. Length of stay in a hotel varies from one to seven days.

It is our policy following a meeting to give gratuities to the people who have done an outstanding job assisting us. Some of these people would be: Convention service people, front desk, sales, bellmen, housekeepers, set up crew, golf pros, and telephone operators. Additionally, we deal with tour operators such as personnel from the hospitality desk, bus dispatchers, drivers and guides.

It is always difficult to know how much each gratuity should be. Any guidelines you could give us would really be appreciated.

Here is an example of how concerned large corporations are about keeping their image. It is not a question of money to most of them, but to have their people who represent them be knowledgeable in how to handle tips for all situations. In this case they want to be assured that all the service people are compensated for the efforts that made their meeting successful. Our response was:

Dear Meeting Administrator:

Many companies, corporations and organizations do not have a tipping system before they contract for services. Up to this point there have not been any guidelines set or rules to follow. The tipping obligations have now gone way beyond what they used to be for a successful meeting, seminar or sales meeting. Tippers International, along with other sources, has established some rules and guidelines to help meeting planners and administrators cope with these unfamiliar situations, in good taste.

The letter went on with information as given in Chapter 9 in this book on Conventions and Meetings.

In the above inquiry, the meeting administrator is looking for guidelines for distributing gratuities to the people who have done outstanding work for a successful meeting. The gratuity in this case would probably be a percentage automatically added to the bill. All this could be contracted before the meeting takes place, but then there is no guarantee that the service received will be good. This would be considered tipping in advance.

In the case of tipping, which is considered a voluntary gift or payment, you have total control over the way the money would be distributed. Those who perform well receive tips and those who do not would receive no tip or a lesser amount. This makes the division of monies more effective.

A New Jersey executive questions the logic of tipping based on the price of the meal:

Gentlemen:

I don't know what your motivations are for establishing this organization or for writing "Guide For Tipping," but I'm very pleased.

One of the few things which gets me upset is tipping. I don't understand it at all. Why should I tip $1.50 for a $10.00 meal and $3.00 for a $20.00 meal? Both involve the same amount of work. I can feel my blood pressure rising. Please send the book quickly. Thanx.

This question is logical and one of many that arises every time you dine out. We answered in this way:

Dear Sir:

> *If you are accustomed to tipping by percentages, it is customary to tip 15% for the smaller amount, but if the prices rise to where the tip seems too large for the service provided, it is proper to tip less, say 12½% or even 10%.*

Other inquiries and questions along this line have been brought to our attention. For example, how is the tipping handled if two or more people are dining out and one person orders a diet meal, with a cost of less than $8.00, and the other orders a larger meal at a cost of $20.00. The waiter handles all the orders and serves them at the same time. Theoretically, the service is the same. It is done at the same time, off the same tray and extra trips are not necessary. But, people are expected to tip according to the amount of the bill. If an average of 15% is used to figure the tip, the $8.00 meal would tip $1.20 and the $20.00 meal would tip $3.00. But, the service was the same. If the bill is divided equally between the diners, an unfair burden is put on the person who ate the cheaper meal and those who ordered more expensive meals would be getting a break.

If dining with a group, it is best to arrange before hand how the bill is to be divided. In a large group, it is sometimes necessary to appoint one person to handle the finances and the tipping. Some people will tip by the percentage method. Others have a policy of tipping an even amount, say one dollar, for each meal served. On a cheaper meal the dollar might mean a tip of 20% or more, and on a higher priced meal the tip might range from 12% to 10% or even less. But, they feel that everything averages out. Also, if the group frequents the same place and has the same waitress, a mutual understanding between the service person and the group could develop and the service would probably be excellent.

Here is a letter of complaint from a Denver waitress.

Tippers International:

> *Just wonder if anyone in your group has ever worked for tips. From the sounds of your ideas, you haven't.*
>
> *Waiting tables is very hard work. Waiters are usually paid less than minimum wage. Our tips are a big part of our income. I've been waiting tables for two years and the average tips are not 15% to 20%, and this is not because of the service. An average tip is 10%. Even when the food was "GREAT" and the service was "GREAT," more often than not, it is 10%, and when there is some kind of problem it is 5% or nothing. Most people are simply not aware of proper restaurant etiquette, and your type of attitude makes things worse.*
>
> *Instead of writing a book on how to tip, why not write a book on the etiquette of being served? Teach people to be nice and helpful to waiters. Help people realize how hard we are working for them. Most importantly, teach them to be nice. When I wait on someone who is nice, I tell them. I just wish this could happen more often. Our society would be much better off if you would simply promote being nice and polite.*

We agree that tipping is a two-way street and complaints about customers are too often valid. Service work in the hospitality industry is an honorable profession and the world cannot get along without the service pros. We responded:

Dear Waitress:

> *We understand and appreciate your comments. Your work in the hospitality industry is very important. However, each profession has its drawbacks and hardships. Because of the nature of your position, it is sometimes impossible to please everyone. All consumers are not alike and their needs vary as much as the service varies from those who serve them.*
>
> *We also realize that being on your feet and on the move is very tiring. But your job also has it compensations.*

You might say that you are in business for yourself, but at no expense to you. You have the chance to work in fine surroundings and to meet many people from all walks of life. You do not have to look for customers, they come to you, and you can either create goodwill or destroy it, depending on your salesmanship. You are generally free to change jobs as you see fit and can increase your income by improving your professionalism as a service person.

From a non-tipper:

To Whom It May Concern:

As for the waiters and the waitresses, why should we pay their wages? That's up to the employer. He should pay the wages they are supposed to get. Nurses, doctors, bankers and many more — they don't get tipped. Tipping is a racket.

Tippers International responds:

Dear Sir:

Similar thoughts have been expressed by many people across the land and around the world. This is the one nice thing about free enterprise and the tipping situation. No one is obligated to tip for any service if they feel they can do without the service or if they feel that service is free. There might be many cases or situations that they are right, but it still remains the choice of each individual to do what they feel is best.

Another member wanted to know about tipping beach boys.

Dear Mr. Schein:

I recently joined Tippers International and received the "Guide for Tipping." There was not mention made of tipping beachboys at resort hotels. Is it appropriate and are there any guidelines?

169

Dear Member:

Not too many people encounter beach boys in their daily lives, but they should be treated and tipped about the same as the waiter or waitress, unless they do special services for you. These people usually have access to special equipment that can make your stay more comfortable. If they help you it is proper to compensate them with tips to suit the service.

We often receive letters with questions about how to tip at buffets, luncheons and group meetings. A typical inquiry is:

Dear T.I.:

What do you tip at buffets or smorgasbords when you do not receive full service? Luncheons, particularly the bridge club variety, also present a similar problem.

Dear Writer:

There is no need to tip for buffet unless you receive some form of table service. If you do, such as coffee pouring, a small gratuity would be appropriate.

For a luncheon, the problems are the same as for any meal. The standard criterion of 15% of the total bill would be best, but the situation of working it out is often not easy. The best thing to do is to talk it over before the luncheon and make a plan on how the money will be handled. Select someone to be responsible for paying the bill. Choose a place that is convenient to everyone, and be sure that gratuities are not already included in the cost before leaving a tip. If gratuities are included, it is not necessary to tip extra, but this add-on does not guarantee the best service. It is important that you compensate according to your club's standards. Never be afraid to check over your bills, and there is nothing wrong with discussing them, but avoid arguments.

Tipping should be discreet and generous. Sometimes groups are hard to serve, and they often hold tables longer than necessary, reducing the service person's potential for more income. Customers should take these things into consideration when determining how much to tip.

Here is an inquiry that expresses the confused feelings a lot of people have about tipping.

Dear Sirs:

Recently a short magazine article caught my eye. The item said, in effect, that most waiters and waitresses are insulted if they do not receive at least 15% of the total bill as a tip, and prefer 20%. I wrote a letter that the magazine published in response, saying that our intent as tippers is not to insult but rather to reward. Indeed, most of us who eat out occasionally can ill afford to tip more than 10%. Usually, though, I am convinced that the amount of the bill should not have so much to do with the size of the tip since it does not require more work to deliver a customer a lobster than it does a beef plate.

Mostly I am writing because tipping bothers me, and when I am out on business trips, I have a tendency to overtip, rather than undertip, and then I am angry with myself afterwards. Indeed, I often tip even when I am disgusted with the service. I guess that you can say that I am a compulsive tipper. Is there any help for me?

P.S. I'm going to New York in two weeks. What shall I do?

Response:

Dear Compulsive Tipper:

I'm sure that waiters and waitresses like the over-tipping you so graciously leave them regardless of the service received. I am sending you the materials you requested. Our philosophy of tipping is "What You Receive is What

You Leave" and the first rule of tipping is "Let the Tip Do the Talking." These should help you to come to grips with tips.

After his trip to New York, our Tippers International office received another letter from the same man that read:

Dear Tippers International:

Thank you for your prompt response to my letter requesting help as a "tipaholic." Your letter and the tipping materials arrived just the day before I left for New York. So, I took everything with me to read while there.

My trip to New York was to attend an institute located about 45 minutes outside the city. However, we spent much of the time in the city where we saw four Broadway plays, took a bus tour of Manhattan, and a boat cruise around Long Island. I tipped our bus tour guide $3.00, although I was the only one who tipped. I tipped in a couple of restaurants, around 10%, but I refused to leave a tip in one high class place, because I, like my compatriots, felt ignored by the waiter.

Already I felt a little more comfortable about tipping. I've read the "Guide for Tipping" and I'll reread it as often as needed for support. Your organization and its goals are sound, and I commend you for them. I will be happy to share the good news with others, and maybe in time we'll all get tipping back into the proper perspective.

My best wishes to you and your fine organization.

CHAPTER 13

***

Providing Good Service

Service is the most important criterion for tipping, but we know that all service is not equal. We also know that all customer requirements are not the same, and that one service person's efforts will satisfy some people, but the same performance does not please others. Here we find a conflict of interest because it becomes necessary for service persons to practice their professionalism in determining the customer's wants and needs. We also find some customers impossible to please, no matter what is done for them.

Ed Solomon, in his book "Service is an Honorable Profession," says that service persons should remember to:

1. Serve your guests in a relaxed manner.
2. Make suggestions whenever possible.
3. Be pleasant and friendly, and provide fast, quality service.

By becoming expert in serving the public, you will develop pride and people will sense that air of confidence about you. Then slowly, but surely, you will realize, as will they, that service is truly an honorable profession.

Restaurant Service Professionals

Service is one of the oldest acts of hospitality and is special to the customer. To your customer, dining time is time for relaxation, conversation and companionship. It is expected that service people be cheerful and friendly to insure the enjoyment of good food by the customers. When someone enters a restaurant, they expect not only fine surroundings, but a gracious hostess to greet them and give them personal attention — "The Customer is King." A restaurant is also the place where people tend to show off their clothes and personalities. A young fellow will often take his date out to dinner to try to impress her. Anyone performing services must be able to feel and be aware of these special occasions.

A warm smile always relaxes the customer, "Good Evening" or "Good Afternoon" is also very effective and the customer's name should also be used if you know it. Customer satisfaction should always be the prime concern of the hostess and all the other service people. The first sign of good service is water on the table, served from the right side of each guest.

As in anything else, the first impression is of utmost importance. Present yourself with a smile, as someone willing to provide cheerful service. Greet customers in such a way that they feel they will get good service. The customer is a guest and should be treated as a personal guest under any conditions.

You should be neat in appearance and have a pleasant and outgoing personality. Personal appearance really counts. In a restaurant, the service person should know the menu, prices, specials of the day, and have knowledge of the foods listed. The table should be properly set so there is no unnecessary interference when people are seated.

Actions speak for themselves. Time should be taken with customers even if it is a busy day. Attention should be divided equally among customers. Again, a smile is helpful for it reflects the mood of the serving person. Sometimes customers are smothered with over attention which makes them feel helpless. Assisting a customer is only necessary when they seem to require help. There are times to be serious and there are other times when kidding around is appreciated. Service people should recognize this and act accordingly.

Customers look for service people to be communicative. They appreciate being spoken to distinctly and in a tone which can be heard, particularly if the room is a little noisy. It helps to smile and look directly at the person with whom you are speaking. Use the titles "sir" and "madam."

It is expected that service people be alert to all the needs of the customer. If information is requested, it should be supplied by the serving people in the most expedient manner. Particular attention should be paid to the needs of small children. Bringing food quickly for children will save much anguish for the children and their parents. Having a children's menu and crayons and paper to entertain the children while they are waiting to be served, lets customers know that family service is appreciated by the restaurants. Kiddie cocktails also show the parents and children that they are important and that their presence is appreciated. Restaurants catering to families should always have high chairs or junior chairs for their little customers.

Use of tact, initiative and cheerfulness is always appreciated. Knowledge is a must, particularly in resort areas. Attention to detail is also a must. Removing of non-essentials should proceed as the program or meal progresses. Your customer's needs should be supplied before they have to ask. Teamwork by the service people shows the great willingness to serve and reflects itself on the establishment.

Maitre d'/Hostess

In most cases, a maitre d' or hostess is in full charge of the dining room area. This person is the key to a successful operation in the dining room. The first impression given is very important in customer satisfaction. The cheerful "hello," the neat appearance, pleasant expression, friendly smile and pleasant voice, will go a long way toward giving a favorable first impression. The maitre d' or hostess should be alert and take nothing for granted. They should follow through on assignments and be alert to customer needs by continuously observing the dining area. It is their responsibility to instill in the service personnel the importance of satisfying the customer, so the customer will praise the fine food, excellent service and warm reception they received.

When the customers are greeted, it is very appropriate for the maitre d' or hostess to ask if they need help with hanging their coats, and offer assistance with packages if they have any. The customers should be led to their seats in a leisurely fashion, because they have come for relaxation. The chair is pulled out for women guests if they are alone or if the man is not assisting. An opened menu should be placed before each guest and the name of their waitress or waiter should be given. The table should always be totally cleared and reset before seating new customers.

Waiter/Waitress

A waiter's or waitress's first concern should be appearance. A smile is of vital importance in appearance. A thorough knowledge of your duties, pleasant attitude and the use of good judgement will help in becoming a good waiter or waitress. Being able to express the willingness to serve is very important. A cheery greeting and a pleasant good-bye will always be remembered. A customer is not always right, but they are never wrong, so the use of tact is always necessary. Being able to make the customer feel at ease is a fine trait and goes a long way toward building a good reputation. Having a happy disposition and pleasant attitude say more than words. Yes, efficient service is always recognized. Proper attire and cleanliness will be a good reason why some people might want you to wait on them. Courtesy, dignity and a charming manner make an excellent service person.

Getting started right

You can start right if you fill the glasses with ice and water. Serve them from the right side of the guest with the right hand. See that customers have menus and make sure that the menus are complete.

Before dinner drinks

If the restaurant serves cocktails, it is proper to ask the customer if they would like a drink, like a martini or manhattan. You should repeat their order verbally as you write it down so there is no chance of error. It is good to know all the ingredients of drinks. When serving cocktails, place the before dinner drink in front of the customer. Again, serve from the right. It is proper to ask if the customer wants the drink mixed. Customers should be allowed to enjoy their drinks, so don't attempt to take their food order at this time unless they ask you to do so. When the customers are about half finished with their drinks, ask them if they would like to order more drinks or order their meals. If a second round is ordered, the empty drink glasses should be removed with the right hand and the second round should be served as you did the first.

If your restaurant serves appetizers, make sure your guests get a good supply. You should be alert as to what their needs are, whether it is another drink or food. You may ask whether they want to relax before you take their dinner order. The decision then will be made by them.

Order Taking

Most of the time when people come to a restaurant, they don't know what they are going to eat until they look at the menu. It is up to the waiter to help the guest decide what to order by making suggestions and offering extras. There are usually a large group of items from which to choose and it is only common sense to realize that no one can be familiar with every item on the menu. It is the duty of the service person to help if requested or needed.

You will usually have either a presold customer or an undecided customer. A presold customer will look quickly at the menu, order the main course and hand the menu back to the waitress or waiter. The serving person must then carry the customer through the rest of the order verbally. The undecided guest will turn to the serving person and ask "What's good today?" or "What would you suggest?" It is always wise to have a good knowledge of specials of the day so you can suggest them first. If this does not work, suggest the most popular items or your preferred items. Lead the customer through the rest of the order. For a guest who might be in a hurry, suggest an item that you know is readily available or does not take long to prepare.

It is very important that you guide the customers very carefully through the meal selection process. The customers should have the opportunity to choose the items they like. Carry them through by asking very simple questions. There is a great difference between being an order taker and a skilled service person. Be very thorough in taking the order, repeating the order to each guest as you write it down. Be very specific and find out how they want their food prepared, especially if beef is ordered. Make sure that all choices are mentioned and ask what beverage they want and when they would like it served. By carefully following through, you will eliminate unnecessary conversation and save time in taking the order. Make suggestions throughout your conversation so that they will realize your concern for their welfare. If a special item is sufficient for one or more, advise them. Also, remember that giving attractive descriptions of suggested items can stimulate their appetites.

Wine

In some restaurants, wine may be a specialty or is available to give the establishment an air of distinction. Wine service is one of the ancient traditions of hospitality. Wine should be used to increase the guest's pleasure and sense of pride in dining out. Wine does lend a touch of elegance to an ordinary meal. It is quite common that customers will order red wine with meat and white wine with fish or poultry. However, the opposite is not unusual. Sometimes one bottle of each is ordered so guests have a choice. (A section defining the specific skills of the wine steward immediately follows this section.)

Serving

If you arrive at the guest's table with food before they have finished their before dinner drinks, reposition the drinks between the water glass and the cup of coffee. All unnecessary glasses should be removed. Again, work from the right side.

When serving dinners, serve those that are most likely to get cold first. Steaks served in hot platters stay hot. The main entrée should always be placed in front of the guest. In serving any meat with a bone, the bone should be to the left so the guest can make his

 first cut directly into the meat. It is a good procedure to check that everyone has the proper knife for eating, steak knife for steak, etc. You should inquire about the type of steak sauce that is preferred and the sauces should be served with caps on to allow the guests to shake the sauce. Continue to remove any unnecessary glassware and dishes. Change ash trays if needed and refill water glasses. The table should be checked for bread and butter.

Beverages should be served at this time to those who requested them with their meal. You should check that the meals are prepared the way the guests wanted them. If, for instance, a steak is not done well enough, return it to the kitchen for additional broiling or replace it if it is overdone.

If there is a complaint about the food, you should know what the policy of the house is. Most places give another choice from the menu to acknowledge the fact that they are there to be of service to you.

Clearing

Never remove the main plate until all the guests in the party are finished, except when requested to do so; or if three or four of the guests have finished and have waited a considerable amount of time for the fourth guest to finish. This does not apply when guests arrived at different times. If a guest leaves a large portion, it is proper to suggest a "doggie bag" so the guest may take the food home.

Side dishes and casseroles may be removed as soon as they are finished. The bread and butter plates should be removed last. The table should be crumbed with a crumber or a napkin with a small plate. All that should remain on the table are water glasses and cups and saucers. Coffee should now be served to those guests who requested it after their meal, and also refill the cups of the other guests. Also, refill water glasses and change ash trays.

Dessert

The guests should be asked if they would like dessert or after dinner drinks, perhaps offering to bring them menus or showing them a dessert cart if the establishment has one. Again, be ready to offer suggestions, especially if there is a house specialty. Repeat the orders back to each guest to be sure that you have correctly understood their order. When the dessert is served, serve from the right and be sure that each guest has the necessary silverware.

The Bill

Before bringing the bill for the meal to the table, double check to make sure that the customer is being charged properly for all items ordered. Discreetly ask who is to receive the bill and wait to see if there are any questions about the bill. The customer may want you to take the bill to the cashier for payment. Promptly return the change and also a receipt if one is requested.

Wine Steward

When the bottle of wine is brought to the table, it should be presented to the host's right side, label up, for inspection. It should not be wrapped in a napkin and it should be wiped clean.

After the host has accepted the bottle, the cork is removed and the top of the bottle is then wiped with a napkin. Bottles of flat wine (wine that is not charged) are placed upright on the table or in a wine basket behind the host's wine glass. Charged wines, such as champagne or sparkling burgundy, should be placed in an ice-packed bucket to the right of the host's elbow, not on the table. The exposed part of the bottle is wrapped with a napkin which acts as a handy grip for the host or waiter. An extra napkin should be folded over the handle of the bucket. This way there is a dry napkin to wipe the bottle and prevent dripping on the table.

180

When wine is served at the table, the glass should be placed on the table half way between the fork and knife. Napkins are only used when serving by the glass. The glass in front of the host is then filled about ¼ full. The host will try the wine and give the sign that the wine meets with approval. Then the guests should be served clockwise, beginning with the first guest on the host's left and continuing until the host has been served again. To be extra special, the host's first glass (tasting glass) may be removed and a fresh glass placed in front of the host. If wine is served with the meal, all wine glasses are placed between the water glass and the coffee cup.

Bellboy

A greeting of "hello" is always welcomed by travelers, whoever they may be. The bellboy should pick up the luggage and direct the guests to their room. In most cases you will first direct them to an elevator which you will locate and operate so they get to the proper floor. During the escort you might be asked questions in regard to entertainment, dining or location of sights. Instruct them accordingly. Your thorough knowledge of the city and the hotel in which you work will be very important. Try to stay up-to-date on the current offerings of local entertainment as well as those restaurants that cater to particular needs. For example, those that cater to families, offer quick service, or leisurely exclusive dining, depending on what the people want.

When you get to the room, check the thermostat, air conditioning or heating. Sometimes the shades are pulled and you should ask if they want them put up. If ice is not in the room, advise them where and how to get the ice. If it is a more exclusive hotel which supplies alcoholic beverages and soft drinks in the room, check the supply. It is also your responsibility to check the towels in the bathroom, particularly when you see there are more than two people in the room. Then ask if there is anything else that they might require. This is providing good service and should earn you a nice tip.

Doorman

A doorman is primarily expected to open doors and this is your routine duty. A service oriented doorman will also help people unload luggage and equipment from their car. You will order their car in advance to be waiting for them at their request. You may provide an umbrella for guests if it is raining and phone for a taxi if necessary. You also can summon a porter or bellboy and watch a guest's car. You control auto traffic, provide security and, most importantly, present a first impression for the hotel.

Taxi Cab Driver

A taxi cab driver can give a considerable amount of special help. You may help in carrying heavy and awkward cases and packages. You may also help carry bags into the building. If requested, you should return to pick up your riders at a specified time and also wait for them if needed. You provide the security that travelers need to enjoy their visits.

Parking Attendant

A parking attendant should deliver an auto as promptly and carefully as possible. If a passenger is a woman, it is expected that you will run around to open and hold her door, not lean across the front seat and open it. If there is a man, you should also hold and then close the door for him. Remember that you are driving other people's cars and therefore are responsible for them. Horseplay is never appropriate in this job.

Golf Caddy

As a caddy, you should always be courteous and call the people you are serving "Mr.," "Sir," or "Madam." You should be very attentive and alert. It is best if your customer advises what is expected of you. This can bring about a more relaxed atmosphere. Give your name so that you can be addressed directly.

Hand your customer the driver on the tee and the putter after he has hit to the green. It is expected that you should be asking if he wants the ball washed; smoothing the sand, when the rake is available, after he has played out of a bunker; tending the flag stick when the ball is on the green and removing it when the ball is close to the hole; and going ahead for a closer watch when a tee shot may reach trouble.

Your customer might want you to help line up a putt, suggest a club, or provide the distance to the green.   Therefore, your knowledge of the course and prior experience are very important. If your customer is playing a "blind" shot over a hill, you may ask if he wants you to give the direction by standing at the point over which the ball must travel, then getting out of the way.

A caddy should never swing the clubs, talk or horseplay with other caddies, or lag behind unnecessarily. You should not rattle the clubs or offer advice unless asked for it.

When the round is over, check the clubs and ask your customer what he wants done with them. If your service as a caddy has been good, your customer's appreciation should be shown by a generous tip.

Latest Review Of Restaurant Service

In an endeavor to give the public the most up-to-date service information, one of the writers planned a trip for the purpose of reviewing 20 restaurants. The restaurants visited were from the good medium class to the ultimate.

We found that the service people who required no tipping, particularly stewardesses and car rental people, treated us excellently, even very late at night. We were very pleased with their pleasant attitudes and willingness to help.

We were somewhat surprised by the choice of hostesses in some of the restaurants. Of 20 restaurants visited, there were three hostesses that were very unfriendly and insensitive to our needs. Yes, even in some very excellent restaurants. We wonder why it is difficult for some people to smile or to be pleasant. Being a hostess is public relations work and if a person does not feel comfortable in that type of work, they should not be involved.

In one restaurant there was a table set for four, but there were only two of us. We requested to be seated so that both of us would have a view of the stream outside. The hostess responded with a glare and a reluctance to help, but we were finally seated as requested. But, all the damage was done. There was no willingness to help, no friendliness or warmth.

The two other unsatisfactory hostesses didn't smile, but just led us straight to the table. There was no pleasant greeting, no conversation, and frankly, no interest in building any goodwill. These restaurants certainly cannot expect to build up any business with these hostesses in charge. Also, where we found the third unsatisfactory hostess we also found an inadequate waitress.

In further review, we found three superior hostesses. Those at the balance of the restaurants ranged from good to very good. The food industry could certainly work to improve this phase of their operations.

In the survey of waiters and waitresses we found that four of the restaurants had excellent waiters and waitresses with whom we could find no faults. Four restaurants ranked very good, six ranked good and the balance were fair or poor. There is no wonder that some people have been disgruntled with tipping. This sampling is small in number, but still shows what an average person might run into when traveling.

In an effort to get as complete a survey as possible, and to present both sides of the story, one of the writers checked restaurants to see what they were doing to improve their services. It was found that some offered a "person of the month" award to encourage better performance by their employees. Others go right to the public for their comments with fill-in questionnaires. Some typical samples are shown below.

Hospitality

1. Were you greeted as you entered?   ___Yes ___No

2. Did the hostess/host seat you?   ___Yes ___No

3. Did server introduce herself/
   himself by name?   ___Yes ___No

4. Were you thanked and invited to return?   ___Yes ___No

5. Do you visit us often?
                   ___First Time ___Occasionally ___Regularly

6. How many were in your party?   _____

Food & Service

1. Was food served promptly?   ___Yes ___No

2. Was your food order correct?   ___Yes ___No

3. Did you receive smiling, courteous service? ___Yes ___No

4. Was food properly prepared?   ___Yes ___No

5. Was hot food served HOT?   ___Yes ___No

6. Did you have
   ___lunch
   ___dinner
   ___snack

7. How would you describe the service?
   ___Just right
   ___Too slow
   ___Too Fast
   ___Other

8. How did the price compare to the food and service?
   ___About right
   ___Overpriced
   ___Lower than expected

Surroundings

1. Was the restaurant clean overall? ___Yes ___No

2. Did your serving staff have a neat and
   clean appearance? ___Yes ___No

3. Were your dining utensils
   and dining area clean? ___Yes ___No

4. Were the restrooms clean
   and properly supplied? ___Yes ___No

Requesting comments and suggestions through the use of forms like these are very positive signs. It is good for the public to respond and to know of the interest taken by the serving profession toward making improvements.

We have found in some of the restaurants that we visited that the waitresses had to take a two week training course. This was very evident in the superior service that was received. We believe that there are efforts being made by the service industry to improve and thereby to bring tipping back to its original concept.

This limited survey is not meant to be conclusive, but the lessons that we all should learn from the review of these 20 restaurants are:

1. The public is looking for good and courteous service.
2. Service establishments should continue to evaluate their people, particularly the people who have direct contact with the public.
3. People will not return to an establishment where they are not treated properly.
4. The serving professionals should continue to strive to improve their personalities, tact, initiative and attitude.
5. "The Customer is King."

CHAPTER 14

***

Amenities For Women

If you ask a waiter or waitress if they give women the same quality service as men, they will probably answer yes, but surveys show that this isn't always true.

Women Concerned About Tipping

The old claim that women are poorer tippers than men may be changing. Women are definitely more concerned about tipping than men these days. A Tippers International analysis shows that approximately 85% of our inquiries for tipping information have come from women. A close study of over 1500 responses indicated that almost 2/3, or 1000, of the responses were from women. Inquiries from women executives, homemakers, teachers, business women and others asked a variety of questions from how to get the same attention in restaurants as men, to how much to tip at a buffet luncheon, to what to tip the bingo runner.

Women On The Move

There was a time when women didn't pay much attention to tipping. Now women are a great portion of the work force. They are traveling more, entertaining more and seem to be experienced with lost luggage, travel delays, and trouble with food service.

Women often receive less attention in the restaurants than men and we believe this will continue until serving people, who, in restaurants, are predominantly women, recognize that times are changing. The best way for women to change their image is to become better tippers. As soon as waiters and waitresses discover that women today are as concerned as men about tipping correctly, the good service will be there. Inexperience is often the root of most tipping problems. Business women can compensate for their lack of travel experience by studying travel magazines, travel guides and also by asking a lot of questions.

Help From The Service Professional

Here we present some of the problems women encounter in their travels. Women often feel they get bad tables for breakfast and that they are waited upon after the men, because the service people feel that the men are busy and must rush off to work. Women feel that it takes longer to check out their credit cards. Car rental agents often assume that a woman is someone's wife. These inequities that exist are being corrected and service persons should do their part in treating women the same as men.

The service professional should respect a woman's special needs and her right to privacy. Bartenders should assist a woman traveler in avoiding harassment, asking her permission before passing a note or serving a drink offered by someone else in the lounge. Women dining alone should be seated at a quiet table, not near the kitchen or in the middle of the room. When a woman checks into a hotel in the company of a man, the desk clerk should not assume that she's the gentleman's wife, secretary or friend. She could be the man's boss, and certainly deserves the same attention as any man!

Many of the problems traveling women have experienced in recent years are a result of their inexperience. Airlines have conducted seminars for airline representatives on helping women travel more easily. One airline published a triannual newsletter especially for female executives.

Hotels Respond To The Traveling Woman's Needs

Surveys indicate that 60% of the business women who travel tend to spend most of their free time in their own rooms. A magazine survey indicates that over 3,000,000 businesswomen spend over 30,000,000 nights each year on the road. This means a lot of rented rooms, so hotels have taken steps to understand and meet the needs of the traveling businesswoman. Some hotels are experimenting with special amenities for the woman traveler by creating all women floors or sections in hotels. These special floors provide some of the special needs that women travelers have, such as blow dryers in the bathrooms, a hospitality suite with honor bar, vanity cases, extra skirt hangers in the closets, women's and business publications, and added security. They also feature rooms with floral decorations and places where businesswomen may meet. Many women still face the problem of having spent a day at all male meetings only to spend a night alone in a hotel room if it is decided not to go out with the boys. So, hotels that provide a warmer atmosphere and comforts are really appreciated.

It is interesting to note that 15-20% of business travelers are women, about five times the number of a decade ago. This is certainly a growing segment of the customers that service people will be serving and this should be recognized by all service professionals. Because women are taking more positions in the business world it is inevitable that more and more business travelers will be women.

Important Statistics About Women

According to reports from the Chamber of Commerce of the United States, more than one-half of American women are working outside of the home. This represents the greatest participation by women in the labor force of any nation in the free world. American women are making great strides in our economy. In one of the last censuses, American women managed over 2,500,000 businesses in this country and this continues to increase. They certainly qualify for service equal in quality to that received by men.

CHAPTER 15

***

Specialized Service
And Information For
Disabled Travelers

The improvements in travel conditions for the disabled have grown enormously in the last five years. Thousands of public areas and private areas are becoming more and more accessible to the disabled traveler. Today, more than ever before, people who are disabled in various ways are moving about and traveling to places all over the world. They are vacationing with their families and attending conventions, seminars and meetings with their fellow workers. We have had considerable personal contact with the disabled which helps us to recognize the great improvements made in this area. However, we still have a long way to go.

Improved Travel Conditions for Disabled

In years past, facilities offered no special conveniences for disabled people. But, in recent years, the public has provided access to nearly all public buildings, with the addition of sidewalk ramps for better mobility and special handrails and facilities in washrooms, to mention a few. Specially marked parking places are provided near buildings for easier access. We also find that most modes of transportation are now providing facilities to help the disabled help themselves. And, of course, the service industry is heavily involved. In many situations service people are able to cope with special conditions because of their training and experience in helping the disabled.

Assisting the disabled is now becoming common practice and most everyone is willing to help. But, this help sometimes is not free of problems. There may be extra fees charged, and, of course, a whole new category of tipping comes into view, possibly increasing the traveling costs. It is best to carefully look for places to visit, stay and dine that offer special services for the disabled person. There are places that provide special rooms designed for the disabled in the hotel's lower level, bathroom facilities that are equipped for disabled people with wide doors and handrails, and wheelchair ramps for easier access to dining rooms.

Disabled persons can also make travel for themselves easier. When packing, take as few clothes as possible and still feel well-dressed. This is good advice for all travelers, but especially for the disabled traveler. Remember that you probably are dependent on someone else to carry your luggage, so the less there is to carry, the better it will be.

Also, don't underestimate the value of a wheelchair. Even if you do not normally use a wheelchair, it can make a difficult trip much easier. Also, you can move much faster and not delay your traveling companions. If you do not own a wheelchair, you can rent one from a surgical supply house. Rent the smallest wheelchair you can fit in comfortably, because you will find it much easier to use.

Tipping For Extra Services

Tipping in hotels, restaurants and on planes, trains, buses and tours should be the same for everyone. There is no need to feel that you have to give larger tips for special services. Most places encourage people to use their special facilities and do not expect extra money for them. Only for special favors and extra services is it necessary to tip. Our advice is "be generous, but discreet."

Hotels And Motels

There are certain hotel and motel chains that should be commended for their efforts in creating facilities for the disabled.

Some hotels have created rooms that are specially equipped for the disabled. Handrail bars around lavatories, tubs and showers, wider entrances, and even restaurant menus in Braille allow visually impaired and other disabled persons to travel with greater ease.

There are lodging directories that indicate which hotels have special rooms for disabled travelers. Tell the hotel management of your special needs when you make your reservation and make sure you get a confirmed reservation when you need a special room. Remember that there are areas that still have older buildings, including hotels which have narrow halls and inappropriate restrooms which can prove to be an obstacle to the disabled person.

Specialized Services

Hotels with specialized services usually have experienced service people accustomed to treating disabled people in a normal way. Advance planning is necessary and highly recommended,  so that upon arrival you will get good service. When you drive up to the hotel, the doorman will take your luggage and turn it over to the bellboy. The doorman will help with the wheelchair or any other service which is necessary. If you have come with an automobile, the doorman will try to contact a parking attendant familiar with hand operated or special driving controls if this is the type of automobile you are driving. The auto will be parked and cared for carefully. It would be proper to tip the doorman a minimum of one dollar for this extra service and the parking attendant about the same.

The bellboy has received your luggage from the doorman and will wait for you to check in at the desk. If any help is required with a wheelchair or any other special equipment, the bellboy will provide it. When you get the room key from the desk clerk, you may give it to the bellboy who will lead you to your room. The bellboy will open the room and show you the special facilities available and how to operate them if you would like. At least a one dollar tip would be in order unless you have more than two bags.

If the hotel or motel has full service and meals are available in the room, a tip of 15% of the bill would be proper for the person delivering the meals.

When checking out, it might be well to phone your schedule to the desk clerk so that when you arrive at the desk the bill is ready to be paid. This would eliminate waiting. The bell captain will assign and make arrangements for your car, cab or bus. Your tipping procedures should be the same as with other places and services. There is no need for you to feel that you have to give larger tips for special services as most places encourage people to use their special facilities and do not expect extra money for them.

Here again, we find the service people to be professional and open to helping disabled persons enjoy their trips.

Cruise Lines

We would like to alert disabled people traveling on cruise lines. Most cruise ships are registered in foreign countries and they feel they are exempt from U.S. statutes because they sail under a foreign flag. There are a number of foreign flagged ships that are now wheelchair accessible.

There was a case where a disabled traveler who could not walk paid a premium price for a wheelchair accessible cabin on a Norwegian cruise line to find one barrier after another throughout the ship. There were obstacles that blocked him from dining in the restaurants, using the restrooms and any emergency evacuation equipment.

Presently there is a lawsuit filed in U.S. Court arguing that cruise lines that cater to Americans, use U.S. ports and sail U.S. waters must conform to U.S. laws by making their ships wheelchair accessible.

The United States is the largest source of business for cruise ships. About 80 percent of cruises depart from North American ports and about 76 percent of the 9.8 billion passengers that cruise ships carry are American. Cruise lines have their headquarters in this country and market to U.S. citizens, so it makes sense that U.S. civil rights laws should apply to these ships.

Air Transportation

Due to recent rulings and court actions, travel restrictions have been eased for disabled travelers. No airline serving in the United States can reasonably refuse passage to a disabled traveler who pays for a ticket and who is of no threat to the safety of other passengers. This ruling has been questioned, however it is a step in the right direction. When you make your reservation, either through a travel agent or direct with the airline, be sure they know the exact nature of your disability. If you need special assistance or a wheelchair, let them know at the time you make your reservation. Then airline personnel will be prepared to assist you when you arrive at the airport, at your final destination, and also at any change points along the way.

Some airlines accept wheelchairs for storage in the cabin and allow blind travelers to keep their canes with them in the cabins. There definitely is a relaxation of rules which apply to the domestic airlines, and many foreign airlines are also accepting the changes.

Airlines are responding to the needs of the disabled in the design of planes. New planes are being designed which offer aisle armrests that fold up to allow a wheelchair passenger easier access to the seat. Lavatories have been designed with wider doors and more inside space with built-in helpful devices such as handrails and accessible faucet and toilet controls.

Airlines are also showing their sensitivity to the disabled by adding handicap assist features when they refurbish planes. On board wheelchairs that can be used to travel up and down the aisles are also being purchased by a few airlines. Motor carts are available at airports to transport disabled people to their transfer points. Always make reservations early. Almost all airlines put a quota on the number of wheelchair travelers they carry on any one flight.

When in airports where walking distances are too much for some people and they need special attention or a wheelchair, there is no cost for these services. If you can handle the wheelchair yourself or even if you have someone push you, it is usually necessary to make some arrangement to help with your luggage. Arrive at the airport at least one hour before departure time, if this is possible. Always make arrangements to go on board before regular passengers. Some airlines have special lifts for boarding. Only for special favors and extra services is it necessary to tip. Here again, "be generous, but discreet."

Automobile Travel

Taxicabs and airport vans are not built to handle wheelchairs. There are a few car rental companies that now make hand controls available at no extra charge on some of their cars. Reservations should be made up to 60 days in advance. In most cases these cars cannot be dropped off at any rental location, but most be returned to the original location.

One of our suggestions would be to equip a recreational vehicle (RV) with the proper controls and equipment for the disabled traveler. This would solve not only the transportation problem, but also the housing problem. The public sector has responded very well in the United States by providing "handicapped only" parking spaces for the disabled driver. This same courtesy is available at most restaurants, museums, theatres and sports facilities.

Plan Your Trip

There are publications and guides available to help disabled people plan their traveling. They may be found in public libraries, tourist offices, tour companies and travel agencies. There have been great improvements in travel conditions for the disabled, but there still are areas of the travel world which need attention. We feel conditions will continue to improve. Plan your trip carefully. Let the places you will be visiting and staying know about your special needs ahead of time. Ask for help.

PART IV

Legal Aspects

CHAPTER 16

***

Taxes And Tips

Service people as well as all other people in a business or a profession have a silent partner — Uncle Sam. We have had discussions with tax people and have reviewed private and government bulletins pertaining to tipping and taxes, so that we could give service people, service establishments and our readers a general report on taxes related to tipping. The Tax Equity and Fiscal Responsibility Act of 1982 (TEFRA) seems to have affected tipping income and taxes immensely. For that reason we have chosen to discuss the tax measures established by this act. To report all tip income has always been the law. The IRS has put greater emphasis on reporting tip income over the past few years because a significant number of taxpayers were not reporting all their tip earnings as taxable income.

The Tax Equity and Fiscal Responsibility Act of 1982 (TEFRA) enacted several measures designed to increase taxpayer compliance. One of the areas they were focusing on was the reporting of tips by restaurants and cocktail lounge employees. It was estimated by the government that only 16% of the taxes on tip income were being paid by service people. To improve on the collections, TEFRA set up a new reporting requirement on qualifying food and beverage establishment employers who had 10 or more employees. They established a tip allocation rule (effective April 1983) to be used when the amount of tip income voluntarily reported by employees to employers falls below eight percent of an establishment's gross receipts.

For the convenience of the service people and establishments required to make reports, we will review the requirements of TEFRA.

Improving Tax Collections On Tip Income

Congress, through the Tax Equity and Fiscal Responsibility Act of 1982 (TEFRA), passed several tax measures for the purpose of more accurate reporting of income. One of the laws was aimed at increasing the efficiency of reporting of tip income by the food and beverage service employees. The government estimates that the new reporting requirements could generate about $1,000,000,000 in additional tax revenue per year.

Under the new law, all reporting, withholding and record keeping requirements remain the same as before, relative to employers and their employees who receive tips. The new law requires a new set of employer reporting obligations. A tip allocation rule was created to stimulate a more accurate reporting of tip income by employees of restaurants and beverage establishments.

Old Reporting of Tip Income

Employees are still required to report to their employers all tips received, equal to $20.00 or more in amount, in any calendar month, on or before the tenth day following the month of receipt. A daily record of their monies received must be kept, and the employees must give their employers a written report of their tips if the total amount exceeds $20.00 in any month.

Employers are still required, as before, to withhold FICA (Federal Insurance Contributions Act) - social security -taxes and income taxes on the tips reported to them by their employees. Some tax people feel that a great weakness exists in this area because the employers who withhold FICA taxes are liable for paying a matching amount. Therefore, the more in tips that are reported by the employees, the more in matching FICA dollars have to be paid by the employer.

The employer may withhold taxes, only to the extent that collection of the tax may be made out of the amount of wages paid to the employee. If the tax amounts exceed the amount of wages paid due to a large tipping income, the excess must be paid by the employee; or by the employer, if the employee voluntarily turned over cash to him to be used for this purpose. The employee's social security tax on tips is always to be deducted first. A written statement must be furnished by the employee showing the amount of the excess.

Highlights Of New Reporting Requirements

The new law focuses upon qualifying large food and beverage employers and sets additional reporting responsibilities upon them. Beginning with the 1983 calendar year, food and beverage organizations which were normally employing 10 or more persons have had to and must continue to file annual information returns.

The annual returns must contain information regarding the amount of income received by the establishments and by its employees for each calendar year.

The return must contain the following:

1. Name and social security number of each employee.

2. The total amount of tips actually received by employees and reported to employers.

3. The total amount of charge receipts on which there were charged tips to employees (other than nonallocable receipts).

4. The total amount the employer is required to report with respect to service charges of less than 10%.

5. The total amount of all receipts taken in by the establishment from providing food and beverages (other than nonallocable receipts).

Many view the new law as basically a reporting measure, but it has varying effects. The new law helps employers by requiring additional reports which help classify their employees into "indirectly tipped" and "directly tipped" categories. This classification is necessary for the application of the new tip allocation rule set upon employers by TEFRA.

Food and beverage establishments must abide by a tip allocation requirement which requires that the excess of eight percent of the establishment's gross receipts over employee reported tips must be allocated among employees who receive tips as income. The employees that are classified as "directly tipped" are the only ones that are subject to the allocation rule. The allocation will not apply if the employees report tips in excess of eight percent of the gross receipts. Further discussion of this subject is under the heading "Tip Income Allocation" near the end of this chapter.

Tippee Reporting Requirements

Tips versus gifts

Cash tips received by employees during their course of employment are considered compensation and are taxable income. If a true gift is received by an individual, it is not considered compensation and is not taxable. If a tip is paid to a waiter or waitress in a form other than cash, like tickets, goods, passes, etc., it is not subject to withholding and is not considered wages or compensation to the person receiving the gift. However, the value of non cash tips, such as tickets, passes or other items of value, are also income and subject to tax. But, do not report the value of any non-cash tips to your employer. You do not pay social security taxes on these tips.

Reporting your tip income correctly is not difficult. You must do three things:
1. Keep a daily tip record
2. Report tips to your employer
3. Report all your tips on your income tax return

Tips are not considered to be gifts because they lack the essential point of a gift which requires that "it is given without claim or demand." Tips, in the past and now, are sums of money given for good service.

It has been interpreted that tips paid to waiters and waitresses are considered compensation and as such are subject to federal income tax and must be included in gross income. Both cash tips and charge tips are subject to the above rule.

Tipping reports to employers

Employees receiving tip income of over $20.00 during one calendar month must report the amount of their tip income to their employer. When tip income totals over $20.00 in a calendar month, it is subject to withholding of income tax and social security, or railroad retirement tax, and must be reported to the employer by the tenth of the following month. If the tenth day falls on a Saturday, Sunday or legal holiday, the report is due on the following day that is not a Saturday, Sunday or legal holiday. However, if an employee receives less than $20.00 in tips while working for one employer during one calendar month, it is not necessary to report this amount to the employer. The employee must, however, record the amount on their federal income tax return. If an employee switches jobs during the month and no one establishment provides more than $20.00 in tips, no report is necessary, even if the total tips of both jobs amounts to over $20.00. But, total amount of tips must be included in annual gross income.

Splitting tips

In some establishments the tips are split with other employees. Tips may be shared with busboys, wine stewards, the maitre d', bartenders, waiters and waitresses. The employee is only required to report the actual amount received and not the amount shared with other employees. Another name for this procedure is Tip-outs.

Service charges

There are times when parties, banquets or other celebrations are held in hotels, restaurants, clubs or halls and a service charge is required for using the facility. If this service charge is turned over to the employees who did the serving, the service charge is not considered a tip. The amount received by each server does not have to be included in their report of tips to the employer, and in turn, the employer does not include this charge in his record of tips. However, this service charge is part of the server's wages paid by the employer and is subject to withholding.

Employees record and report of tips — IRS Forms 4070 and 4070A

It is recommended that all employees keep a daily record of all tips received. This can be done very easily on IRS Form 4070A. It must be remembered to also record any tips received in a tip splitting arrangement. This record in turn can be used as a guide to fill out the Employee's Report of Tips to Employer, IRS Form 4070.

It is very important that the employees save their copies of the daily record of tips like any other income tax papers. Under the new regulations, employees (if audited) may be required to prove why and how they might have received tips, if the amount reported is less than eight percent of the establishment's gross receipts. If accurate records of tip income are not kept, employees may be subject to penalties. If records are lost or not kept, and sufficient substantiation of amounts cannot be made, the IRS might make a determination based upon experience in a given locality. The tax liability that is computed at that time by the IRS must be proved erroneous by the taxpayer.

Why it is an advantage to report all your tips

1. Unemployment compensation payments are determined by actual payroll records. If you become unemployed, you can

only draw according to what your employer's records show in wages and tips.

2. In case of accident, and you have disability insurance, the insurer will compute the loss of income solely on your payroll records.

3. When you retire, the social security payments are based on your contributions. If you pay less now, you will get less later.

4. Not all fellow employees on your team in the same establishment receive tips. They report their full income and pay their full share of taxes. It is unfair to them if you do not do the same. They have made it possible for you to receive tips.

Withholding By Employers Of Tippee's Tax

Employers must withhold from wages, social security taxes and any other income taxes that are due on the tips reported by the employees. The exception would be if the employee had no income tax liability the previous year and does not expect any for the current year. The employer will not withhold any income taxes from the wages of an employee if a completed Form W-4 (Employee's Withholding Allowance Certificate) requesting exemption is provided. A new Form W-4 must be filed each year by February 15 in order to renew the exemption. Penalties for filing false W-4 forms are very severe. The filer could be subject to criminal prosecution.

There must be legitimate reasons for exemptions. It must be shown that the employee did not owe any federal income tax for the previous year and had a right to a refund of income tax withheld, the employee does not expect to owe any tax for the current year, and also expects that all tax withheld will be refunded.

The employer will continue to withhold social security taxes from the wages of the employee subject to these taxes even if an exemption from withholding of income taxes is filed.

Failure To Report Tip Income

Under-reporting of tip income can prove to be very costly. A penalty equal to 50% of the employee's social security tax may be assessed on an employee for failing to report income from tips. This penalty is added to the tax owing on the unreported amount. Any employee who receives $20.00 or more in tips in a one month period must report this amount to his employer. If the entire amount of tips was not reported to the employer, then the employee must figure the amount of social security tax on the amount of tip income that was not reported. When the employee is filing their income tax return they should use IRS Form 4137 (Computation of Social Security Tax on Unreported Tip Income) and attach it to Form 1040. All tips received must be included in the income shown on Form 1040.

It might be tempting for some service people to under-report the amount of tips they receive, because any additional tip income reported to the employer will increase the amount of tax the employer must withhold from wages. The wages of waiters and waitresses in general are traditionally low, and some do not receive the minimum wage per hour, so they consider their tips to be their principal source of income. Any additional withholding by the employer from their wages results in lower paychecks being paid. There may even be instances when there is no wage in the paycheck and the employer may expect repayment from the employee to cover any FICA (Federal Insurance Contributions Act) deduction that might have been made.

Failure to report the exact amount of tips is not the solution, especially with the heavy penalties that employees must pay for under-reporting.

Employer Reporting

Employers, in the past and present, are required to withhold social security taxes and any income taxes that are due on the amount of tips that were reported. These taxes are deducted from the regular wages paid to employees unless an exemption from withholding was filed. An estimated amount may be withheld from the employee's wages to cover the taxes to avoid future hardship for the employee and also provide for easier bookkeeping.

Quarterly returns of income and social security taxes on wages must be filed by employers. They use forms 941 (Employers Quarterly Federal Tax Return) and 941A (Continuation Sheet for Schedule A of Forms 941, 941-M, 941SS, or 943 Report of Wages Taxable Under the Federal Insurance Contributions Act).

The employer must furnish an annual Form W-2 to each employee and must include in the total wages the amount of tips the employee has reported. The employer must also furnish a form, Notice 55, informing the employees who have tip income that the amount shown as "Uncollected Employee Tax on Tips" on Form W-2 must be shown on Form 1040 when they file their income tax return. The employee must file Form 1040, reporting and paying the amount of the uncollected tax.

Employers, under the new regulations of TEFRA, must now report the total amount of charged tips shown on the charge receipts and they are required to list to whom those tips were paid.

To achieve greater compliance among tipped restaurant employees, TEFRA has set up information reporting programs for employers of large food and beverage establishments. This information is designed to assist the IRS in the review of returns filed by these employees. Qualifying food and beverage establishments, such as cocktail lounges and restaurants usually employing 10 or more persons, must file an annual information return, IRS Form 8027. If an employer has more than one operation and he conducts activities that provide food and/or beverages at more than one location, it is considered that each location is a separate operation for purposes of tip reporting rules.

Tip Income Allocation

Employers of qualifying food and beverage establishments with 10 or more employees have to determine whether, for reporting purposes, they would allocate an amount equal to the excess of eight percent of the establishment's gross receipts over the total amount reported as tips among the employees who receive tips.

This type of allocation would not have to be necessary if:

1. the employer shows that the average tip rate for his employees is les than eight percent, or

2. all the employer's service people receiving tips voluntarily report tips equal to at least eight percent of gross receipts.

If the employee tip income reports to the employer total less than eight percent, the employer must advise the IRS of the information and estimate the amount of tip income received by the employees who fell short of the percentage.

The percentage of gross receipts allocated may be lowered from eight to as low as five percent upon the employer's written request to the IRS Director. It is up to the district director to determine the amount of percentage of gross receipts to be used for tip allocation based upon the application for reduction.

Allocations are made on a basis of an allocation formula or on a good faith agreement between employees and employers. The allocation formula is based on the proportion of the employee's share of the entire amount of tips received by all other employees receiving tips in the establishment. This only applies to the "directly tipped" employees. In no way will an employer incur any liability in any disputes of employee allocation.

The allocation of tip income which is being discussed applies for reporting purposes only. No withholding of income and social security taxes on these allocated tips are necessary to be made by the employer, because they are merely allocated. The employer withholds taxes on tips that are reported by the employee's W-2 Form as a separate entry. Depending on an individual's situation, the amount of tips that are included in an employee's gross income may be higher or lower than the allocation amount. The IRS makes the final determination on tip allocations.

Good Faith Agreement

What is it? It is an agreement used for allocation of tipped income. It is a written agreement approved by the employer and by at least 2/3 of the tipped employees in each occupation, like waiters, waitresses, busboys and bartenders, in the qualifying establishment. This applies whether the employees are directly or indirectly tipped.

This agreement should:

1. provide for the allocation of the amount which is equitable to all tipped employees,

2. be renewed on a yearly basis,

3. be accepted when the establishment has tipped employees employed in each occupational category affected by the agreement,

4. allow for revoking of the agreement by a written agreement adopted by at least 50% of the tipped employees involved in the agreement.

The Tip Rate Determination/Education Program (TRDA) was developed in 1995 to help those employees receiving tip income and their employers understand the laws on reporting tip income. Under this program, and depending on your specific business, your employee may enter into one of the two arrangmenets – the Tip Rate Determination Agreement (TRDA) or the Tip Reporting Alternative Commitment (TRAC) (created in June 1995).

Currently, the TRDA is only available to the food and beverage industry and the gaming (casino) industry. At this time, TRAC is open to the food and beverage industry and the hair styling industry.

You are required to file your federal tax returns. You may be asked to sign a Tipped Employee Participation Agreement proclaiming that you are participating in the program. The employer, as a participant in the TRDA, has agreed with the IRS to a tip rate for the employer's establishment. To stay a participating employee, you must report tips at or above the tip rate determined by the agreement. Furthermore, as a part of the TRDA arrangement, the employer is required to report your name, social security number, the hours worked or sales made, your job classification, and your reported tips to the IRS if you do not report tips at or above the determined tip rate.

Treasury Department Study

It was reported that, prior to TEFRA, roughly 84% of the taxes on tip income were not paid by the serving public. The Treasury Department has made a study and is following up on the stricter enforcement measures of tip reporting.

The Treasury Department has determined the portion of minimum wage payments that compose tip income. Other results expected are better classification, part-time and full-time employees, tip sharing and tip pooling arrangements. All this information has been very useful for recording data of the service industry as well as providing better means of tax collection.

CHAPTER 17

***

Economic Impact Of Tipping

We should not for one minute underestimate the economic impact of tipping. It is additional income for millions of people. In Chapter 16 we mentioned the fact that the government estimates that by the new reporting requirements of TEFRA they will be able to collect about $1,000,000,000 in additional tax revenue each year. This only applies to the tip income of food and beverage employees.

What is the total tipping income? No one really knows because it would take years of research to get this figure. Tippers International roughly estimates that the tip income for the food and beverage service industry may be about $3,500,000,000 to $6,500,000,000. This figure would be closer to $7,500,000,000 or $8,500,000,000 if tip income in all service industries is included. This means that about $20,000,000 is spent for tipping every day!

Let's just for a minute consider a moratorium on tipping. What would be the results? Immediately, there would be less money in circulation. There would probably be chaos in the service industry because a great imbalance would develop. Yes, a slight recession would even be a possibility.

We feel that the service providers would never slip in their performance so much as to warrant a moratorium on tipping. However, service professionals must continuously strive toward improvement. Our hopes at Prime Consultants continue to be very optimistic that service professionals will continue to provide good service and that they will be justly rewarded.

Yes, we subsidize some of the service industries by tipping. But, if we didn't, the extra wages would have to come from the consumer, one way or another. Would you rather pay more for your food, hotel room, etc. to cover the services? Our survey indicates "no" by an overwhelming majority.

Often, the first impression of a tip is that it is like a tax that is not enforceable. You have the prerogative to choose the amount to pay or even to not pay at all. We cannot say that restaurants are making a "bundle" on us as customers because, if you check the business records, you will find that restaurants have been subject to more bankruptcies than any other business.

We should feel good to have the choice of judging how well a serving person has done for us. If you want to prove something to yourself, just go out for an evening and observe. You will find, as we have, that most serving people are there to serve and please their customers. With the publication of this book, and the efforts of Tippers International and its members, there will be continued efforts toward improvements.

You should feel that you can walk into a restaurant or hotel, and, so to speak, have people working for you. You should be given the impression that "The Customer is King." Serving people realize that they are working for you, the customer. But, the service professional should also be treated with courtesy. There, of course, are times where there will be slip-ups. Only remember the good things and you will realize self-satisfaction in your role as the customer. There is a joy in giving because you can feel that you are helping someone directly. You never get that feeling in paying a service charge.

Tippers are of various incomes and standards of living. Serving people should recognize this fact. Therefore, the amount of the tip is not necessarily the final criteria used to judge the service. The size of a tip may also be based on the customer's ability to pay. The serving professional should always keep in mind the spirit in which the tip is given. For example, a family of six eating out on a special occasion may not be able to afford to pay the size of tip that they feel their waiter or waitress has earned.

We have written this book as unbiased as possible, showing how to handle all tipping situations. We know that after reading this book you will feel better because you will understand and have a broader knowledge of tipping. Let's all continue to tip properly, so service charges will not become prevalent. Tipping is something which has been in existence for centuries, is a part of our culture, and most likely, will continue for a long time. Respect for each other is what we hope to achieve.

INDEX